Deborah Fowler began writing short stories when she was seventeen and has written ever since. Twelve years ago she gave up a career in commerce to write full-time. She has written small business guide books with her accountant husband Alan, and also five novels.

Early in 1989, Alan and Deborah and their eldest daughter Lucy, travelled to Bucharest and after tortuous delays with red-tape were able to adopt Michael, from Orphanage No 4, who is now a healthy, lively four-year-old. The couple have four other children and live in a small village outside Oxford.

OPTIMA

A Guide to Adoption

The other road to parenthood

DEBORAH FOWLER

FOREWORD BY JILLY COOPER

An OPTIMA book

First published in Great Britain by Optima in 1993

Copyright © Shepherd's Keep Studio

The moral right of the author has been asserted.

All rights reserved.
No part of this publication may be reproduced, stored in a retrieval system, or transmitted, in any form or by any means, without the prior permission in writing of the publisher, nor be otherwise circulated in any form of binding or cover other than that in which it is published and without a similar condition including this condition being imposed on the subsequent purchaser.

A CIP catalogue record for this book is available from the British Library.

ISBN 0 356 21012 X

Typeset in Sabon by Solidus (Bristol) Limited
Printed and bound in Great Britain by
Clays Ltd, St. Ives plc

Optima Books
A Division of
Little, Brown and Company (UK) Limited
165 Great Dover Street
London SE1 4YA

For Michael

*With lots of love
from*

Mum

Not flesh of my flesh
nor bone of my bone
But still miraculously my own
Do not forget, not for one single minute,
That you were born
Not under my heart
But in it.

Anon

Contents

Acknowledgements ix
Foreword by Jilly Cooper 1
Introduction 3

SECTION 1 The preliminaries

1 The decision – what circumstances could lead you to consider adoption? 9
2 What sort of people can adopt? 24
3 Personal assessment 37
4 The official assessment 48
5 Children available for adoption 66
6 The financial aspects of adoption 78

SECTION 2 Types of adoption

7 Adopting babies and toddlers 93
8 Adopting school age children 107
9 Adopting older children and teenagers 120
10 Adopting a disabled child 132
11 Adopting a family group 138
12 Inter-racial adoption 149
13 Adopting a sexually abused child 155

SECTION 3 Living with adoption

14	Inter-country adoption	163
15	When things go right – bonding and learning to give and receive love	176
16	When things go wrong – the breakdown of placements	185
17	Your adopted child and his origins – how to tell a child he is adopted	193
18	Tracing	207

SECTION 4 – Fostering

19	Why foster?	221
20	How to become a foster parent	227

CONCLUSION

Useful addresses	235
Useful books for adopted children	240
Index	241

Acknowledgements

I received a great deal of help with the writing of this book – from natural and adoptive parents, social workers, self-help organizations and, of course, from adopted children themselves.

I would particularly like to thank Jane Allan, former Acting Head of Adoption and Fostering for Oxfordshire County Council who was my chief adviser, and without whose help I would certainly have floundered.

I would also like to thank: Martin Berry, for his legal advice; Aunty Vi, for her typing; Margaret Wiltshire, for keeping the children at bay while I worked; and last but by no means least, my husband, Alan, for his wonderful support and excellent spelling.

Authors note

I have found myself in the usual dilemma as to whether to refer to children throughout the book as 'he' or 'she'. The result is I have used both, which I hope you will not find too confusing.

Foreword

This is a wonderful book, both reassuring and realistic. Deborah Fowler has experienced all the excitement, the heartbreak, the agonies of waiting, the restrictions of red tape, the setbacks, and the ultimate, wonderfully worthwhile joys of adopting a child.

Anyone who is either thinking or in the process of adopting a baby, or as a mother thinking of giving up her baby for adoption, or any child who has been adopted, should read *A Guide to Adoption*. Anyone also who wants to read about the human condition and love and pain and fulfilment should read this book.

Adopting our own two children, Felix and Emily, now 24 and 23, has been the most enriching experience of my life. Even when I first held them in my arms, as tiny babies, and felt that first overwhelming surge of love, I never dreamed the extent of the happiness, comfort and laughter they would bring me. Knowing that Deborah has been through all these experiences herself in her search and final bringing into the family of her Romanian baby makes her particularly well-suited to write this book. In our turbulent world there are so many sad, lost children and so many sad parents longing to have children of their own, this book seems a wonderful way of helping them to come together.

Jilly Cooper

Introduction

Adoption is a word which tends to symbolize the last resort of the childless. If confronted with the anguish of infertility, if all medical treatment fails, then adoption is the only remaining option.

This book aims to look at adoption from a completely different angle. Not for one moment am I underestimating or dismissing the terrible grief and suffering experienced by childless couples, nor the importance of the role of adoption in their lives. However, I believe society should turn this view of adoption on its head and consider adoption, not as a solution to a problem, but as a problem in its own right, which needs our urgent attention. To paraphrase President John F. Kennedy, we should not be saying *what can the abandoned child do for us but what can we do for the abandoned child.*

In this country there are many thousands of children living in children's homes or in temporary foster care who desperately need permanent homes. Very few of them are babies or toddlers and very few of them are without some sort of problem – whether emotional, mental or physical. But just as these children come in all sorts of shapes, sizes and ages, so do prospective adoptive parents. The Social Services' attitude towards what makes a suitable adoptive family has changed radically in recent years. Once adoption was something which only happened to babies, and adoptive parents had to fall into the category of a conventional young, married couple with prospects. All this has gone forever – you might be a couple past child-bearing age or living together with no wish to marry, you may be a single woman or man, of any race, from any social background ... If you genuinely want to help a child and can demonstrate your ability to give appropriate care and support, then the chances are that your application will be very seriously considered. There are so many children in this country desperately needing permanent homes, but for some strange reason their plight receives very little general publicity.

And then there are the children in the rest of the world ...

We all wept three years ago when our television screens showed Ceauşescu's legacy – the orphanages of Romania where the children were dying not just from lack of food and care, but above all from lack of love. This human catastrophe made many people think for the first time about adopting from abroad. At the moment the rules on inter-country adoption are a mess, but it is possible to adopt a child from a number of countries. The suffering of Romania's abandoned children is bad enough – in Chile unwanted newborn babies are left to die in concrete bunkers, in Brazil the street children are shot like vermin ... Adopting a child from abroad cannot solve the problems of that child's country of origin. Nonetheless, you can certainly solve the problems of that one child, the child you choose to love: and one child saved is a triumph.

What I am asking you to consider, therefore, is that adoption is not something simply for the childless. If you love children, if you have room in your hearts and in your home for a child, then maybe adoption is an alternative to bringing yet another child into the world. We are bombarded daily with depressing news as to the future of the world. The bomb, amazingly, is no longer considered a serious threat, the destruction of the world's rain forests is a symbol of a bigger malaise – it is the human population explosion which could ultimately destroy this planet. Why bring more children into the world, when so many already here are suffering and dying?

If we are ever to see ourselves as citizens of the world then the more we know about one another's cultures, creeds and colours, the better. I believe there to be a positive advantage in mixing up races and cultures; for black to adopt white and white to adopt black; to not consider every mixed-race child a black child; to not frown on adoption from such places as India and Sri Lanka because of the colour of the children's skin. Maybe it is a naïve view but we are all God's children and the sooner we concentrate on our similarities, rather than our differences, the sooner we will be taking major steps towards making the world a safer and more humanitarian place.

If you believe that adoption (or fostering) either from home or abroad could be for you, then this book will tell you how to set about it, looking in depth at the joys and pitfalls involved. Adoption is not an easy option – many couples who have experienced both the birth of 'home grown' children as well as adoption, are quick to confirm that the drama of pregnancy and childbirth pales into insignificance compared with the anguish and uncertainty of the adoption process. If properly prepared for and carefully considered, however, the rewards from adopting a child can be wonderful – for everyone concerned. Even if you feel adoption is not for you – and it certainly is not for everyone – this book may well change your attitude to the subject.

Please don't turn your back – it is your problem, too, and the need is so great.

DEBORAH FOWLER
Oxford 1993

SECTION 1
The preliminaries

1

The decision – what circumstances could lead you to consider adoption

Adoption means caring for someone else's child. It is important to say this right at the beginning, because however much you love your adopted child and even if you have had him with you from his first few days of life, you did not create him. Someone else did. Extraordinarily, as happens in many adoptions, the child may grow to look like you or your partner, he may have the same mannerisms, share the same interests, views and ideals. The rearing of your adopted child may be a wonderful experience, your relationship as near perfect as any child/parent relationship can be ... but you still will be raising someone else's child.

This then is the stumbling block for many couples who might otherwise seriously consider adoption. They feel that there is some special magic about the bond of blood, that they could not love a child who is not theirs – at least not enough theirs. My eldest stepson is of this view. He and his wife have a two-year-old son and have been advised for various medical reasons that it is not sensible to have another child. My stepson loves his son very much indeed and feels that it would not be fair to consider adoption because he is confident that he could never care for someone else's child as much as he does his own. He is probably right. It would be quite wrong for me in the context of this book (or for your friends, relatives or partner) to try and change your view if this is how you, too, feel. All I can do is to relate my own experience. I have two children by birth and one by adoption. Like every parent I love my children differently because they are different, but I can honestly say that the *degree* of loving is the same for all the children. I would cheerfully go to the stake for each of them. That feeling of love and protection, mingled with guilt and inadequacy, terror and triumph, the awe inspiring swings of emotion which one feels as a parent, are there for my adoptive son and always have been, from the very first moment I met him.

Your attitude to the idea of adoption must be the starting point for your decision. There are many reasons why you might be considering adoption and we will look at these in detail in a moment. Firstly, though, you need to decide whether you are likely to view your role as adoptive parent to be in any way inferior or second-rate compared with that of a natural parent. Is this something you have come to as a last resort, as the only option? If so, you need to be very cautious about proceeding. For most people having a baby is a relatively easy thing to achieve. Adopting a baby is not. Whether the child is a baby or an adolescent, whether the child comes from the UK or from abroad, the whole procedure is fraught with drama, difficult to achieve and wearing on the nerves. Adoption is not something you enter into light-heartedly, you have to feel very positive about it. You have to really want to do it, really believe it is the right move for you and your family, and this can only be achieved by a great deal of soul-searching, discussion and counselling – there are no snap decisions involved in adoption.

Let us now consider the various motives which might make you consider adoption in the first place.

1. INFERTILITY

The traditional reason for wishing to adopt a child is because you and your partner are unable to have one of your own. To reach the point of deciding to try for adoption probably will have meant a long and rocky road of deep unhappiness and frustration. Young people marry, and even in today's wicked old world, see themselves mostly in the traditional role of loving partners and ultimately parents. With women more involved in their careers, it is often not for several years after marriage that a couple seriously consider starting a family. It comes as a terrible shock, of course, when a pregnancy does not follow on to order. Next there is a weary and distressing trek around specialists and consultants to find out whose 'fault' it is, and what can be done to remedy the situation – hope springs eternal. There will be embarrassing and painful treatments until eventually, one day, you and your partner will find yourself sitting before a consultant who says that in his view there is little or no chance of you ever having a child of your own. Disbelief, pain, humiliation, anger, the destruction of a dream – couples cope with their loss in different ways. Some never recover, become increasingly bitter and even find that their relationship cannot stand the disappointment. Other throw themselves into some form of work or hobby. For some though, the pursuit of parenthood remains an obsession, a dream which *has* to be realized for their health, happiness and sanity.

Your feelings may be a mixture of the above, but do not worry if your initial reaction to the concept of adoption is very tentative. Over the months or years of trying to start a family, you will have built up a very powerful image of the baby you desperately hope to create between you. You will have lived out in your imagination various scenarios of how the baby will be, what he will look like, where he will go to school, the likely reaction of your friends and family, what colour you will paint the nursery ... The fantasies – for sadly this is what they have proved to be – cannot simply be banished from your mind overnight – you lived and breathed them, they kept you sane during all the dark days of frustration and disappointment. It is small wonder that you cannot instantly equate in your mind the baby that you feel you lost with the alternative – adoption.

If you embarked on your attempt at parenthood relatively late in life – say, your early thirties, the chances are that by the time infertility is proved, you will be too old to adopt a baby in the UK. You will be advised by the adoption agencies that you might well be eligible to adopt a school-age child or possibly a toddler or a baby with a severe handicap of uncertain prognosis. The alternative is to adopt from abroad, in which case, assuming you are approved for adoption, you may well be able to have your baby. However, in addition to the fact that the baby will not be yours by birth, it will also be foreign, possibly of a different skin colour, coming from a strange culture, from a country you may never have even visited before. Obviously you will need time to adjust to this vastly different concept. You need to mourn the death of one image of parenthood before you embark on another – you must allow yourself time to breathe before you can make the adjustment. In some instances people are so desperate to become parents that they ricochet off the news of their infertility, into being prepared to care for a child ... any child. It may seem strange to you but adoption agencies feel far more confident on balance about tentative couples, the people who need reassurance that they could make good adoptive parents, than the latter group who feel sure that they can cope with anything and just want to get on with it.

So, if you are feeling shell-shocked and perhaps seriously lacking in confidence as the result of the news of your infertility, then it is perfectly all right to approach an adoption agency with all your tentative feelings about adoption and learn as much as you can before making a final decision. As I say, it is far more realistic and reassuring from their point of view, than you being too sure of yourself. Just give yourself time and use that time to learn as much as you can about adoption.

2. ALTRUISTIC REASONS

Your wish to help a child in need, of course, cannot be anything other than an excellent motive for adoption. It may stem from a religious commitment or simply a feeling that life has treated you well and that you want to put something back. You do need to be careful, though. Wishing to help could take the form of a hefty donation to a charitable organization, or hours of voluntary work. Adoption is a very different sort of commitment. For a start, it lasts a lifetime – twenty-four hours a day, seven days a week ... forever. While you may be very moved by hearing of the plight of children caught in some disaster, and you may wish desperately to help, you do need to be cautious if this is your sole reason for wishing to adopt. It may seem an odd thing to say but you do need to have some selfish reason as well – in other words, a balance. You also need a tinge of realism in your idealistic desire to help.

Perhaps, as a mother, you have had two desperate pregnancies or a very bad experience in labour and cannot face the thought of another confinement; perhaps you would like another child but feel you are too old to start again with a baby; perhaps there is some medical problem in your family which makes it unwise for you to have any children. There are countless possible personal motives, any one of which will help balance the scales. This view is not mine alone, it is how the adoption agencies view applications. The problem with pure altruism is that it can be linked to a desire to project a particular image of self-sacrifice. Of course there are many wonderful unselfish, dedicated people who always put their fellow man before themselves, but there is also a tendency for the pious to be rather keen on self-image and there is no place for self-image in the adoption process. *The primary concern must be for the child and the child's welfare.*

It might be helpful here to quote my own family's case history, which I hope will demonstrate the point.

We are a large family – three older children, of which the youngest is nearly eighteen and then three little ones, boys of three and four and a baby girl. The three-year-old, Charlie, is ours by birth, the four-year-old, Michael, ours by adoption and we are fostering the baby, Edita, in the hope of adopting her. I gave birth to Charlie when I was forty-two and my husband fifty-five – by anyone's standards, we were elderly parents. Soon after Charlie's birth we recognized that while it was lovely for us to have a little 'after thought', we were perhaps being rather selfish to Charlie. We live in a fairly isolated hamlet in Oxfordshire, where there are no other young children and we realized that Charlie would be growing up very much an only child. Taking a deep breath, we decided to have one more baby, but it was no easy choice. I'd had a difficult pregnancy and, of course, at my age there was the very real risk of a Downs syndrome child. While still in the throws of the decision, Nicholae Ceauşescu, the President of Romania, was shot dead by his people, and for the first time, the world learnt of the orphanages of Romania. We found Michael in Orphanage No 4 in Bucharest, on 16th June 1990. He was two years old and could neither walk, talk nor stand. We made our commitment to him on that day, and the process that had brought us to him had encompassed an odd mix of emotions and motives. Like most people we had been desperately moved by the plight of the Romanian children and had wanted to do something tangible to help. What drove us beyond simply contributing to the local village fund raising appeal was our own personal need to have another child. In other words, our decision was based partly on selfish and partly on unselfish reasons. What is fascinating now is our reaction to the altruistic part of our decision process. Both Alan and I are enormously irritated when people, learning of Michael's origins, tell us how wonderful we are, how caring, how Christian. We feel we are enormously privileged to have Michael as our son. We consider that the good fortune is as much ours as his. We feel quite simply that we are better people for knowing him and we owe him a great deal. In other words we are no long captivated by the concept but by the person. We, quite simply, have fallen in love – not with an idea of helping an abandoned child, but with a little boy. The same applies to our baby daughter, who comes from Bosnia.

Please do not feel that I am trying to knock the desire to help, far from it. It is what the world desperately needs – more selfless caring. All I am saying is that in order to take on a child for life, there should be some other aspect to your decision process.

3. PERSONAL EXPERIENCE

A fair number of people who decide they would like to adopt a child, do so because of their own personal experience – because they, too, have been adopted or have lost a family, or in some way can relate to the experiences of a particular child. In itself this is an excellent motive for wishing to adopt and such parents can make superb adoptive parents because they can have empathy with the children more readily than parents from a conventional background. Perhaps you yourself have a sibling who has Downs syndrome which has given you a unique insight into the condition. In turn you may feel that you wish to adopt a Downs syndrome child because you have so much to offer it.

The one aspect to guard against is the need to be needed. Sometimes people will have spent all their life in a caring role – caring for younger siblings or elderly parents or someone disabled within their family group. When they lose this role through death or a change of circumstances, they desperately need to find an alternative and *this in itself is not a good motive for adoption*. Once again, your personal experiences need to be combined with some other reason for wishing to adopt.

4. PRACTICAL MOTIVES

Because it is such an emotive subject, on the face of it, it seems appropriate to have strong personal reasons for wishing to adopt. In theory, to take the breezy, practical view that you have the space, the energy and the finance to have more children in your family, does not seem quite right. In practice, however, there is nothing wrong with feeling like this. It may be that you have several children of your own and feel that in an overcrowded world, rather than add to your family by birth, you would like to adopt, and feel materially equipped to do so. This is fine. Perhaps you and your partner are on second marriages, perhaps you have stepchildren but would like to share a child between you. Perhaps because of age or for any of the other motives mentioned above, adoption seems a viable option. This is fine – you don't need to demonstrate endless soul-searching or wearing your heart on your sleeve. Heaven knows, there will be plenty of emotion around when you find your special child. Do not be afraid of being frank with yourself and with adoption agency staff if your true motive is one of practicality.

5. BEREAVEMENT

If parents lose a much loved child, particularly one that lived beyond infancy, then agencies tend to be very worried about the emotional health of the parents and their motives for adoption. As they see it, there is a serious danger of wishing to replace the dead child, of placing unconscious pressure on the adoptive child to fill the space left by death. There is no doubt about it that experience of parenting is invaluable when it comes to adoption. Most adoptions involve children who have been damaged to some degree and it is hugely helpful to have some practical experience to fall back on as you deal with the inevitable crises that will arise. I would therefore have thought that most couples who have loved and lost would make excellent adoptive parents and while, of course, it is important to make sure that they have come to terms with that loss first, it certainly should not be a negative factor.

> *My grandmother was born in the early 1870s. Her second child pulled a saucepan of boiling water over his head, when he was three. It took him three weeks to die. She had him at home, there were no facilities to nurse such children in hospital in those days. He was buried in a cemetery a few miles from the house she lived in until well into her nineties. She had another two children – a boy (my father) and a girl. She raised her three children and then adopted and brought up a grandson. She was a very strong character, quite fierce at times, but her children worshipped her. She was a wonderful mother and grandmother and I will always treasure my memories of her. Up until a few months before she died, she visited the cemetery where her son was buried every single week, as she had done since the day he died. She mourned him for over seventy years but that in no way diminished her ability to be a splendid mother to her other children.*

Like all human experiences, grief can be a very positive thing. It can broaden one's understanding of people and life, put one's priorities in perspective and make one appreciate what one has. If you have lost a child and, for whatever reason, consider adoption preferable to having another child, then you will have to work quite hard to persuade an agency that you have the right motives. If you are happy with what you are doing, then fight tooth and nail for what you believe in because you probably have a great deal to offer.

6. FILLING THE GAPS

If, like ours, your family has some big age gaps between the children, it is tempting to think that perhaps you could adopt to fill those gaps – instant siblings for your children. Adoption agencies are not very keen on this as a motive, at least not as a sole motive, and the concept of filling gaps does not really fit in with the average child's needs. It is very difficult to adopt a child who is older than your existing children. The older adopted child's initial unruly behaviour may well spin off on the younger ones. Before you know where you are, your once happy family is a hot bed of trouble and strife. On the whole, policy in this country dictates that it is best for adopted children to be the youngest in the family. Having said that, adopted older children can work, as is demonstrated by this case history:

Sarah and Jamie had two children of their own, both boys, before they considered the question of adoption. They went to spend the weekend with some friends, who Sarah had known in her student days. Their friends had not been able to have children and so had recently adopted two children – a three-year-old first and then a nine-month-old baby. The weekend had a profound affect on Sarah and Jamie. On the way home in the car, Sarah said she could think of nothing else but how their friends had been able to help these two children, whose lives had been in such tatters. Far into the night she and

Jamie discussed it. They hoped to have a big family and indeed were planning another pregnancy. Suddenly, they began to query what they were doing and wondered whether adoption might be an alternative. They contacted the Social Services and after much discussion, counselling and a home-study they were approved as adoptive parents. Their children, Richard and William were really pleased about the concept of adoption, but Richard, the eldest, was adamant that what he wanted was an older brother. This was not at all what Sarah and Jamie had in mind. Just over a year after their fateful weekend visit, they adopted a little girl of three, followed, two years later, by another little girl of two and a half. Three years later, the family was joined by Freddie, a son by birth. While all this was going on, Richard remained adamant that what he really wanted was an elder brother but Sarah and Jamie did not really take his request seriously. The one thing they were sure about was that as the eldest child in a family of five, whatever else they did by way of increasing their family, they should protect Richard's position. This view, of course, was shared by the Social Services.

About eighteen months after the birth of their last child, their social worker contacted them to say that the elder brother of the second little girl they had adopted was now in care and although the two children had hardly spent any time together, the birth mother had asked whether it would be possible for them to be together. The social worker had felt obliged to pass on the mother's request but did not seriously expect Sarah and Jamie to act upon it. The boy, Tom, was eleven at the time, two years older than Richard. Sarah and Jamie agonized about it for some time. It seemed awful that brother and sister should not be reunited, but at the same time they were very worried about Richard and his position in the family. He was a very sensitive child, who worried a great deal about his work at school and altogether took life too seriously for Sarah and Jamie's liking. They felt that in many ways Richard had grown up too fast, and he apparently had very few friends of his own age.

After much thought, Sarah and Jamie decided to ask Richard how he felt about it. He was absolutely over the moon and insisted that they should try and adopt Tom. With enormous trepidation, and after many formalities and much shaking of the head on the part of their social worker, it was agreed that Tom should be fostered by them while they saw how everybody settled in. The effect of Tom's arrival on Richard was instant and extraordinary. Suddenly he relaxed. It was as if the weight of the world was taken off his shoulders. He had someone to look up to, someone bigger than him, ahead of him at school, someone to show him the ropes. He became less tense, much more open and friendly and suddenly hugely popular, bringing home endless friends, to the point where Sarah felt she was running a café rather than a home. As for Tom, having been the eldest in his birth family, he settled into the role with relish. After a few weeks, Sarah and Jamie had no doubts that Tom had come home.

Richard had been right all along. He had recognized – which neither his parents nor the social worker had done – that he was not really suitable material for being the eldest child of a large family. He found it too daunting to always be the biggest, the one in charge.

Tom was adopted two years later and he and his natural sister have established a special and touching bond. The outcome is a happy one for all concerned.

7. EXPERIENCE

It may be that you have some specific professional or personal experience of disability or, say, racial issues – in other words a particular background which equips you precisely for the adoption of a certain type of child. It could be that you are a special needs teacher, or have a nursing or medical background. Perhaps you are of mixed parentage or there is some form of trans-racial adoption within your extended family. This sort of experience could provide a perfect background for certain types of adoptions. To fully understand the extent of the problems you will encounter by adopting a child with a specific condition is of enormous value to you, to the child and, of course, is very reassuring for your social worker. Once again though, your experience should only represent one aspect of your reason for adoption. For example, someone who has perhaps devoted much of her working life to children with a specific medical condition should not feel compelled to adopt a child who suffers in this way, just because she knows how to cope and recognizes that the need is great. She should not feel guilty about having children of her own or adopting children who quite specifically do not have the problem which is present in her everyday working life. For this reason few social workers adopt or foster. Having coped all day with the problems of damaged, abused and neglected children, in most instances it is vital that they do not meet the same problems on arriving home.

So far as racial issues are concerned, if you are of mixed parentage, it is obviously of enormous value to your adopted child if he or she is the same. At the moment mixed-race children are regarded as black and are rarely, if ever, placed with white couples. This is particularly strange because statistically, most mixed relationships are between white women and black men, so had the child been brought up by the natural mother, he would have been in a white environment anyway. Attitudes to this policy may change, and in my view not before time.

These then are the main motives which might lead you to consider adoption. I would strongly recommend that you do as much research as you possibly can on the subject before making a decision. Read everything and contact all organizations which have literature and expertise available, again look under the section of useful addresses at the back of the book. Organizations such as BAAF (The British Agency for Adoption and Fostering) have very useful booklets which are well worth reading, as do the Parent and Parent Information on Adoptive Services. Make sure that you and your partner obtain as much information as you can, and if possible talk to families who have adopted children. This is particularly useful if you are considering adoption from abroad, as the special problems associated with a child from another country do need serious consideration. When you feel you have built up at least a little understanding of what is involved and although daunted, you are ready to take the next step, then your first port of call should be either your Social Services Department or a recognized adoption agency. As I stressed at the beginning of this chapter, do not worry if your ideas are still not completely formulated – all agencies are used to tentative inquiries and would actually prefer them to the over confident ones. As with the background to any big decision, research is never time wasted – after all the job you are contemplating is a job for life.

2

What sort of people can adopt?

Having made your decision to pursue the possibility of an adoption there are a number of approaches you can make. Assuming it is your intention to try and adopt a child from the UK, you can either apply to the Social Services Department in your area or to a recognized adoption agency. Adoption agencies can be found in most counties and often they have some links with the church. Most agencies work very closely with the Social Services Department and all dip into the same pool of available children. The exceptions to this are certain religious agencies – Roman Catholic and Jewish spring to mind – who deal exclusively with parents and children of a religion or race. Whether you decide to go to the Social Services or to an individual agency is purely a matter of choice. The majority of children are placed by the Social Services. If you are applying to adopt a child from the UK, the procedure for obtaining approval from them is entirely free, whereas some agencies do charge a fee. Whether that fee means that you will receive a better degree of personal attention is largely a matter of conjecture.

Certainly I would recommend that if, for any reason, you do not feel comfortable with the social worker allocated to your particular case, it might be worthwhile seeking an agency as an alternative. If you are adopting from abroad, again there are special agencies who deal with this, but we will deal with this aspect fully in Chapter Fourteen on inter-country adoption.

Regardless of whether you apply to your local authority or to an independent agency, the procedure for selection is the same. All agencies will undertake what is known as a 'home study' in order to assess your suitability to be an adoptive parent. Let us consider the types of people who might apply.

1. HETEROSEXUAL MARRIED COUPLE

A heterosexual married couple, whether in a first or subsequent marriage, obviously in many respects are the ideal – whether they have existing children in the household, children living elsewhere or are childless. Agencies will seek to establish that the marriage is a stable one and that applicants are not trying to introduce a child into a shaky relationship in order to try to resolve their own problems. However the nature of the home study process – which is very rigorous – will almost certainly expose this and other such problems. The couple do not need to have had any experience of children, though obviously some level of contact or knowledge would be seen as desirable.

2. HETEROSEXUAL UNMARRIED COUPLES

Currently, under the law, only one partner can adopt if the

couple are unmarried. Because, for some reason, the partners have opted to remain unmarried, there will be considerable focus of attention placed on the stability of the relationship. However, provided the relationship *is* a stable one, then being unmarried is not detrimental to receiving approval. A couple, though, will need to work out their feelings about only one partner being eligible to adopt. Here again, some experience with children is desirable, but not mandatory.

3. SINGLE WOMEN

Many single women have proved to be very successful adoptive parents. The absence of a partner may actually reduce the complexity of a relationship which can be associated with jealousy. Certain children do need an exclusive one-to-one relationship in order to form a bond and cope with the problems they have experienced. In the case of single people generally, agencies will wish to explore why they are single and the emotional and practical support networks which are available for both the child and the parent, on a day-to-day basis – and, of course, the safeguards available in the event of the parent's death.

Barbara's story demonstrates the type of single woman who should find it possible to be approved for adoption.

Barbara was in her very early forties when she decided she would like to adopt a child. She had never married and although there had been one or two long standing relationships in her life, she had always lived alone, or in a flat with friends. She had trained as a nurse and then specialized in paediatrics. She had recently been left a small legacy by an uncle which gave her financial security for the first time. It was really this factor that prompted her into the decision, recognizing that she would probably now never marry although she had always really wanted a child of her own. Both Barbara's parents were dead, but she had a sister who was married with three sons living locally to her, and an unmarried brother.

It was an advertisement in a PPIAS magazine which made Barbara take the plunge and contact her Social Services. The social worker appointed to her case helped Barbara identify the child she was best suited to care for and eventually Barbara was approved to adopt a child between seven and eleven years old, preferably a girl.

About eighteen months after Barbara's application she was matched with a little girl named Anne, who was eight years old. Anne was the third child of four children and had been sexually abused by her father and neglected by her mother, who was of very low intelligence. She had been in care for three years and had been fostered by a single woman, which everyone felt made Barbara's application that much more appropriate. There were big social differences though. Anne was living in a council house in Leeds, whereas Barbara had a very nice Victorian town house in Pimlico, South West London. Everyone was naturally worried as to how Anne would adapt. The placement was not without problems. Anne had a very low opinion of herself and was very much a non-achiever, needing constant stimulation. Barbara took her role very seriously and went to great pains to understand as much as she could about Anne's past – even visiting Anne's father in prison. Two years on, mother and daughter have settled down into a very happy, workable family life. Undoubtedly in Barbara's favour was the fact that she had considerable experience of caring for young children and the fact that her motivation to adopt was triggered by the simple, practical reason of suddenly having financial security. It is possible that her social worker might not have been so enthusiastic had it been that Barbara was perhaps on the rebound from a relationship which had gone wrong and was looking for some sort of emotional outlet. In addition, Barbara's sister provided the sort of support network that is considered fairly essential for a single parent.

4. SINGLE MEN

Very few agencies will recruit single men, although there have been notable exceptions. As with single women, the agency will seek to establish why there is single status. Is it by choice or because of lack of opportunity to marry, or perhaps separation, divorce or death? Agencies will be very rigorous in their attempts to find the true motivation behind the wish to adopt. I am not saying it is impossible for a single man to adopt but it probably would help enormously if he had some specific experience of children, perhaps with particular types of children.

5. HOMOSEXUAL COUPLES

All agencies are very cautious about placing children with homosexual couples, though they are marginally more confident about lesbian couples. Most agencies are adopting a 'sitting on the fence' position, despite a growing pressure to address the issue. There has been a considerable amount of press coverage on this issue and while there is pressure for a more open view as to the suitability of homosexual couples, there is also a strong lobby which supports the view that a happily married heterosexual couple, with experience of raising children, has to be the best possible choice.

As I mentioned in my introduction, adoption should not be a service to childless couples and this applies whether they are heterosexual or homosexual. Acting in the best interests of the child is of paramount importance, and in most instances placement with a homosexual couple will not fulfil this requirement.

As well as the type of person you are, there are many other governing factors which will affect your eligibility to adopt. Let us look at these.

1. AGE

The only stringent age constraints relate to straightforward baby placements, and have been introduced as a consequence of market forces. In other words, the supply of babies is exceeded by the demand. So far as placing all other children are concerned, agencies will normally apply common sense principles, based broadly on what could happen naturally. In other words children should be placed with adults who *could* be their natural parents and obviously it is important to ensure as far as possible, that a child can be seen through to adulthood by one, ideally, both parents, to avoid exposure to further separation, by death. For this reason couples in their forties and fifties are only going to be eligible for children from school age upwards, which is fair enough ... though there can be exceptions. Perhaps the reuniting of siblings would involve parents being able to adopt a child who is slightly younger than would normally be considered for them. So much depends on the individual parent, and child.

> *Mollie and Brian are now both in their late forties. Brian is a teacher at the local Polytechnic and Mollie is a primary school teacher. In their late twenties they discovered that Mollie could not have children and as a result two children were placed with them for adoption as babies – a boy and a girl, Bob and Tessa, now in their late teens. When Tessa was nine, Mollie and Brian realized that they were becoming increasingly broody and approached their social worker to see whether it would be possible for them to adopt any more children. The result was amazingly three more children, over a period of six years.*
>
> *Two of the children, both girls, had mothers with a history of schizophrenia. The older girl, Jennie, was placed with Mollie and Brian at eighteen months, and Becky, three years later, at the age of two. Finally, just last year Mollie and Brian adopted Simon. Simon was the result of a concealed pregnancy of an under-age mother, who had delivered the baby alone. The child received no medical attention for twenty-two hours, having been left in a bus shelter, in a bin liner. As a result, it was felt likely that Simon would suffer from some development problems, and indeed he is already displaying a degree of learning difficulty. Nonetheless all three children are thriving.*
>
> *The reason that Mollie and Brian were able to adopt such young children, bearing in mind their ages, was because of the uncertainty relating to the background of each child. It was felt that an older and experienced couple would be more able to accept the prospect of*

whatever problems might lie ahead, and discussions took place with consultants and specialists in relation to each child, before a decision was made to proceed. It is in these cases, where children are considered to be 'hard to place', that very often older parents can be the best answer.

It is also important to mention here that older couples *can* adopt babies and toddlers from abroad. Some countries put an age restriction on adoptive parents but most do not – more of this in Chapter 14 on inter-country adoption.

2. AGE OF CHILDREN ALREADY IN THE FAMILY

As a general rule, agencies like to avoid creating what could not happen naturally. There are always exceptions to this rule, as well, but generally agencies prefer to introduce adopted children as the youngest in the family to avoid, as far as possible, the potential for jealousy and imbalance of attention, and an upset as to the status of any children already in the family.

3. PERSONAL STATUS

There are no golden rules as to what is considered suitable with regard to employment, housing, financial position, religious, political or indeed lifestyle issues. Different parents suit different children, and what may seem a slightly bizarre family in the scheme of things, could be ideal for a particular child. Nonetheless, the tedious aspects of making ends meet and keeping a roof over one's head, all contribute to the general stability and well-being of the family as a whole, and it is these details which agencies look at closely. In other words, you do not have to be middle-class and of substantial means to be considered a suitable adoptive parent – quite the contrary – but you do need to be relatively stable, and this applies not only to the practical aspects of your life, but also to the emotional. Being out of work has a bad effect on self-esteem and if you, as a potential adoptive parent, are feeling insecure and have a poor sense of morale, then you are obviously not an ideal candidate. So, by using the word 'status' I stress you do not need to demonstrate an exotic lifestyle. In fact I know I have agencies' backing in saying that they would be far more impressed with a shabby little house which has been romped in by children over the years, than they would be by a perfect baronial hall, with not a Ming vase out of place, and in all probability, a sterile, loveless atmosphere to go with it.

4. PERSONAL QUALITIES

The personal qualities which are most vital are as follows:

- Above all it is important to have an openness – to others, to ideas, to the wider community, to criticism. A narrow attitude will worry agencies considerably.

- You need to be able to demonstrate the capacity to think and learn from the experience of others. You should not be too blinkered, or proud to accept advice.

- You should be slow to judge.

- You need to have the imaginative ability to put yourself

in the shoes of the child and indeed, the child's birth parents, to really understand how the child is likely to feel and, therefore, how to cope with those feelings.

- You must not be a prima donna, you must have the ability to work in partnership with the Social Services or agency and with your social worker in particular.

- You must be an advocate for children, and you must be on the children's side. Above all you must *like* them.

- Flexibility – you will need a great deal of this.

- Humour – you will need a bucketload of this.

- Stamina and determination – if you do not have these qualities in a fairly concentrated form, you will probably be destroyed by the system long before you even meet a prospective adoptive child.

- It is also necessary to have a fairly high level of self-esteem. This does not mean that you should believe you are always right, but if you do not have some confidence in yourself and your own abilities, you will not have the courage of your convictions to carry through what you have set out to do.

5. PERSONAL CIRCUMSTANCES

There are certain circumstances relating to your past that automatically exclude you from consideration.

- Offenders – obviously all offenders against children or

those with a history of repeated violence, or a pattern of recurrent and constant offending in any particular field, are considered inappropriate as prospective adoptive parents.

- Personal experience of abuse – this can be a positive factor or it may well be a negative one. So much depends on your current attitude as to what has happened to you. It is a sad fact that the abused often go on themselves to abuse.

- Separations – if you have already demonstrated an inability to sustain relationships, it is likely that you will be eliminated from consideration. In other words, if you have been through a great many marriages or partnerships, or if you have been unable to maintain the role of parent with any previous children, then this will undoubtedly count against you.

- Medical conditions – all applicants are required to have a full medical, similar to that which is required for insurance purposes. Each agency will have a medical adviser who will consider your particular case. The children who are available for adoption will have already been through a great deal and as far as possible, it is important to be sure that they are not going to lose you once they have found you.

- Psychiatric illness – if you are a diagnosed schizophrenic or you have a personality disorder, or you have had a number of hospital admissions for psychiatric related problems, then it is unlikely that you will be considered. However, periods of reactive depression, particularly those which might have resulted from your infertility, will not necessarily be counted against you. It depends, of course, on the severity of the depression and over what length of period. However, provided that there are strong reasons for the condition, then depression in itself should not exclude you from consideration.

- Physical illness – serious illness such as Parkinsons disease or multiple sclerosis, indeed any incapacitating disease, with the implication of increasing dependency or shortened life expectancy, would eliminate you from the possibility of being considered as an adoptive parent. Even former illnesses will be considered carefully – a previous heart condition, now controlled or cancer apparently cured, will be very carefully investigated, to try and assess likely life expectancy.

Of course, all of the conditions listed above are strictly commonsense. If you recognize for whatever reason, that you may not be eligible to be an adoptive parent, please do not try and withhold information from your agency. The home study process, which assesses your suitability, is so rigorous that it is extremely unlikely that you will be able to suppress information about a serious problem. However, even if you do find a formula for 'getting away with it' and are not concerned with the moral implications of this, your secret will haunt you for ever and will be a constant source of stress. The children who are available for adoption – both in this country and the world over – have been through a very great deal of hardship, abuse, malnutrition, neglect and abandonment in various degrees of severity. As a result, they deserve the very best when it comes to starting a new life. None of us if perfect. We have all had our fair share of problems and all too often take the wrong turnings in life – what you need is strong motivation and a lifestyle which can offer the love, stability and comfort which should be every child's right.

3

Personal assessment

Home studies, these days are pretty rigorous – in fact some people would say, far too much so. Adoption agencies, in their search for adoptive parents, could well be accused of making the assessment too idealistic, expecting too much of us – who are, after all, just ordinary people with our own share of faults and problems. Nonetheless, this is the system which prevails at the moment, and although attitudes to adoption are likely to change in the next few years, it is important that you are as well prepared as possible for the whole process.

It seems a good idea, therefore, that in advance of making your approach to an adoption agency, you first undertake with your partner (if appropriate) your own personal assessment. I am not suggesting you do this in order to try and come up with the 'right answers' to the home study questions – in fact, quite the contrary. What I am suggesting you do is to take a long, careful look at yourself and your motivation, to reassure *yourself* as to your suitability. This process will be helpful in many ways to clarify your thinking. Perhaps most important of all, it will give you the confidence to press your case if first you have convinced yourself that this is something you really *want* and *can* do. The home study process can be very daunting. Without appearing arrogant, it will be helpful if you can demonstrate a well-founded self assurance. I see your personal assessment being divided into five major headings:

- Attitudes

- Lifestyle

- Experience

- Support network

- Expectations

Let us deal with each of these in turn.

1. ATTITUDES

One of the most vital requirements of the prospective adoptive parent is an attitude of **tolerance** – general social tolerance to drugs, drink, race, sexual behaviour... It is no good being judgemental, it is no good having fixed ideas as to how people should or should not behave. Yes, of course you must have your own code for living, your own code of ethics, which suits you. However, what is right for you is not necessarily right for everyone. Like any parent, adoptive parents must mould and guide the children in their care, but, nonetheless, they must respect each child for what he or she is. Some of the things that the child stands for you may not like – you may even abhor. Perhaps your child is the product of an incestuous union; perhaps your child was abused; perhaps your child's birth mother is a drug addict or a prostitute. Most adoptive children carry with them a horror story, and that horror story cannot be swept under the carpet. You have to accept it and live with it, because it is a part of your child. *And you cannot live with it if you are sitting in judgement over it.* That old expression 'hate the sin, not the sinner' is perhaps the most appropriate piece of advice here. You must not bring up your little daughter to hate her birth father, because he sexually abused her. You must bring her up to hate what he did to her – probably because the same thing was done to him when he was a child and if so, you can explain that he was a victim, too. Tolerance is not something you can fake. You can cover up your disapproval on social occasions when you feel you are on display, but within the body of the home, your prejudices are bound to show.

Hand in hand with tolerance goes **flexibility**. With a child who is likely to have been damaged, it is very important to set fairly stringent rules and to have a code of discipline to which you stick. Nonetheless, your child is likely to change a very great deal in the first months and years spent with you. Many children will regress, needing to behave like babies or toddlers, to act out the childhood they feel they never had. Others will need to express their anger and hurt which has been building up over the years, and this may take the form of some very violent behaviour. These are simply stages that all children go through, but in an adopted child they will be more intense, and you will need to be on the ball in order to keep up with them, and to amend the rules as the child changes and develops. Nothing, so far as the raising of a child is concerned, is writ in pillars of stone – everything needs reviewing from time to time. What applies to children also applies to your lifestyle.

More on lifestyle in a moment, but you do need a very flexible attitude as to how you run your life, once that life includes an adopted child or children.

Pride is something you cannot afford to have. You need to be able to ask for help and not be too proud to accept that sometimes you will be presented with a problem with which you cannot cope. This may mean, of course, going back to your social worker, health visitor or doctor, or it may be more appropriate to look to you partner or extended family. You must not be too heroic because, not only will you suffer, but so will your child. Adopting a child is not easy and you must accept that sometimes you will need to be helped. Asking for help does not put your role as an adoptive parent in jeopardy. On the contrary, your social worker will welcome it.

It goes without saying that **humour** is a very necessary attribute. You have to be able to laugh at yourself and teach your children to do the same. Taking yourself too seriously, apart from anything else, makes life dreadfully dull – for yourself and for those around you. Humour can be a great diffuser of tension. One moment the family is in crisis, the next, the right chance remark can have everybody in hysterics of laughter. Humour is a vital tool to any parent.

Finally and perhaps most important of all, you and your partner need to discuss at length your attitude to the **roles** you will be playing as parents. One of you will be the main carer. Will this be a full-time job or will the main carer undertake some part-time work? How much support can the main carer expect from the other partner? Will there be any resentment if the answer is 'not very much'? In other words, you need to explore your own personal attitudes towards the caring process, both in practical and emotional terms.

2. LIFESTYLE

Every childcare book will tell you what a huge impact the birth of a baby will have upon new parents, and this is true. Nonetheless, most couples have nine months to prepare for the event, the mother will be stuffed full of appropriate hormones to help her bond with the child, and the new little person at least will sleep for a good deal of the time, initially. Adoption can and often is far more daunting, particularly if you are adopting an older child. Yes, school will take the strain up to a point, but there are weekends and holidays to consider. It is very easy to find that caring for an adopted child, particularly one who has been severely damaged, is a twenty-four-hour/seven-day-a-week job, and quite rightly so, if this is what the child needs. Life really never will be the same again – the lie-ins on Sunday morning, jolly pub lunches, trips to the cinema/theatre ... whatever your particular fancy, it is likely to go by the board. You will be exhausted, the house will be a mess, you will never have five minutes to yourself, your appearance will go to pot and your social life with it. I am sorry if I am sounding so negative but I am thinking specifically of the early days of adjustment. Of course, once you and the children are all used to one another, things will gradually settle down ... *but they will never, never be as they were.*

Perhaps the question you should ask yourself is what you would NOT be prepared to give up in order to adopt a child. Is there any aspect of your life that you simply must maintain which is likely to be under threat if you have a child to care for? If so, you need to have a very long, hard think before going ahead. This problem, of course, could centre round your work. Adoption agencies are not averse to parents working (up to a point) but at least one partner will need a fairly part-time job or be prepared to give up work altogether in the early months of adjustment. So far as the main carer is concerned (which usually will be the mother), she needs to recognize that work will not, and should not, be the priority in the future. Yes, it may be important to her but it has to play second fiddle to her role as a parent. If she is not prepared to do this, then she should not be adopting.

Very often, by the time a couple have been through infertility treatment, they are not particularly young. Here again the older one gets, the more intractable one becomes, and the more difficult it is to adjust. You may be very comfortable in your home, enjoy your nice ornaments, silk cushions, cream carpets or whatever. On the face of it, these seem to be fairly minor considerations but in fact they are not. The trappings of life are very important to most people, and undoubtedly will be under threat with the arrival of a child on the scene. You need to be absolutely sure that not only can you cope with the adjustments necessary, but equally important that they will cause no resentment.

How you live is also an important factor. As a childless couple, do you live with a high degree of order? If so, that orderliness will be under seige. Alternatively, do you live a relaxed, unstructured life? In these circumstances there may be less to destroy but a complete lack of structure does not provide a child with the right environment in which to thrive, particularly if that child is very damaged and insecure. Are you prepared, and are you able, to change the very pattern of your life, to bring a routine and sense of order to it, or relax your standards – whichever is appropriate?

Many parents, particularly adopting older children, find that the time they spend alone as a couple becomes minimal, and this may be particularly difficult when they are under stress. A close loving relationship needs fuelling in order to stay healthy and this may be very hard to achieve, particularly in the early days.

Much of what I have said may seem very obvious but I think it would be true to say that most prospective first-time parents do under-estimate the impact that a child will have upon their lifestyle, whether they are adopting that child or giving birth to it. If possible, try to spend some time with friends who have children about the age of the child or children you are proposing to adopt. Study how they live and see whether you could bear to live in the same way. Of course everybody's approach to parenthood is different but there will be many aspects which are unavoidable. Answer the question – can you *really* cope?

3. EXPERIENCE

For many, if not most, prospective adoptive parents, their future adoption will be their first experience of parenthood. Normally adoption agencies do look for reassurance that prospective parents have had some knowledge of children and their ways. Perhaps they have nieces and nephews or younger brothers and sisters. If this is not so in your case, then it does not preclude you from being considered as an adoptive parent. Everyone recognizes that often the first time a woman ever holds a baby is when she holds her own.

Lack of experience is particularly not a problem when the prospective parents are aware of their shortcomings. If within your extended family you have no small children, it is difficult to gain experience in a natural way. It may be that you are a God-parent or have close friends with a small child, in which case taking a particular interest in him would be very useful. This may seem an extreme suggestion but sitting in a children's playground, watching them playing and inter-acting together, can be very rewarding and useful. You should also consider watching selective children's television programmes and reading some good children's literature. An author for example such as Roald Dahl, had the ability to think as a child does.

Inevitably, as someone with little experience of children, you will not feel very confident about prospective parenthood and this will be made more difficult by the fact that, in many instances, you will be adopting a child with severe problems, whether emotional or physical. Experienced parents do find it much easier to put things in perspective. I know in my own case, when my adoptive son used to throw very bad tantrums, I would have been far more worried about him if I'd had no other children. As it was, I knew he was behaving in just the same way as they had done during the 'terrible twos'.

If you are considering adopting a child with special needs, then I would suggest it is vital that you try and find someone who cares for a child with a similar condition so that you can really appreciate fully just what problems are involved.

As I have said, experience in itself is not a prerequisite for adoption but it does help. Far more important than trying to persuade an adoption agency as to your ability to cope, is acquiring the confidence from having obtained as much experience as possible.

4. SUPPORT NETWORK

What kind of support are you likely to enjoy from your family and friends? Looking first close to home – does your partner go away from home on business trips for protracted periods, or commute long distances, so that you will be left on your own with your new adopted child for long periods? Will you be able to cope? How about grandparents – how will they feel about your adopting? Then there are your friends, your neighbours ... Jenny's case may seem extreme but many adoptive parents suffer degrees of this problem

> *A friend of mine, Jenny, adopted two children because she and her husband were unable to have children of their own. The infertility problem was hers, not her husband, Harry's. Harry's mother never let Jenny forget it. There were constant references to Jenny denying the family the opportunity of continuing the blood line. Every time the children behaved badly, there were references made to their origins. It was a nightmare situation and in the end Jenny and Harry only overcame it by banning Harry's mother from their house, which was very sad for all concerned.*

You may find that the older generation, particularly, are less amenable to the concept of adoption, on the grounds that family is family and blood is thicker than water, etc., etc. The extended family should not influence your decision if you and your partner are committed to the concept, but, nonetheless, you need to be aware of the problems you are likely to face and not be hurt when the criticisms start to flow. Inevitably, adoptive parents can be very hypersensitive and overprotective.

It would be sensible in this context, therefore, to check out how family and friends will feel, so that if there is any hostility, at least you will be prepared for it. On a practical note, if you are a single parent contemplating adoption, it would certainly be an enormous help to your case if you can demonstrate that in the event of your death, the extended family would take responsibility for the child. In other words, for the single parent a support group is a necessity, rather than just an advantage.

> *I interviewed recently a single woman named Barbara, who had adopted a Downs Syndrome girl called Mary, when the child was eleven. The Social Services in charge of the case had been very reassured by the fact that Barbara had a married sister ten years younger than her. Barbara's sister had undertaken not only formal guardianship of Mary in the event of Barbara's death, but had made it clear she would welcome the child to live as a member of her family full-time, recognizing it to be a commitment for life. Do not panic if this sort of arrangement is not available to you as a single parent, as it is only one consideration among many. Nonetheless, it is something that you should think about.*

5. EXPECTATIONS

As I mentioned in an earlier chapter, when a couple decide to have a child, inevitably they build up images of that child – what the child will look like, what skills the child will have. Will he be practical like you or a thinker like me ... ? that sort of thing. Men really do dream about their sons playing cricket for England, and women of their daughters being cosy companions for life, and there is nothing wrong with all of that. Where it goes wrong is if these expectations put pressure on the child. To force a child into a role which is not suitable for him but which allows the parent to act out his or her own fantasies is sadly not an uncommon occurrence. Unrealistic ambitions are more likely to exist with an adopted child. By definition the children who are available for adoption either in the UK or from abroad come from some sort of traumatized background. In many cases this means that their deprived family circumstances may result in learning difficulties which may stand out in stark contrast to their parents' own achievements, and/or ambitions. This in turn may make it very difficult for the parents to relate to the child's problems. Children coming from abroad particularly may be the product of generations of malnutrition and neglect, with resultant physical and psychological problems. Enormous achievements can be made by these children in the right loving background, but those achievements may well fall short of what the parents might consider to be 'normal'. If you feel you are somebody who might be unrealistically ambitious for your adoptive child, you need to look at your reasons for adopting very long and hard. Are you looking for some sort of reflective glory from your role as a parent, because if so your motives could be genuinely suspect?

I am sorry if once again I appear to be playing the devil's advocate, but the questions I have put to you in this chapter are only the sort of questions that will be addressed by the social worker undertaking your home study. If you and your partner have had an opportunity to talk through these particular areas of concern, at least you will be less flumoxed at the interview.

4

The official assessment

The procedure for the official assessment follows the same basic pattern throughout the UK, and in this chapter we will follow them through.

1. THE INFORMATION MEETING

Whether you apply to adopt directly through the Social Services or from a voluntary agency, the procedure is likely to be the same. Once you have made your approach to what I shall refer to as 'the agency', the first thing which is likely to happen is that you will be invited to attend an information meeting. These are held at regular intervals – some encompass all prospective substitute carers – ie., prospective adopters *and* foster carers, but in most instances the meeting you will be expected to attend will be targeted specifically at adopters.

At that meeting, information will be provided as to the kind of children available in your area, and the procedure it will be necessary for you to go through in order to adopt a child. If you are quite specifically wishing to adopt a baby, you will be warned of the long time delay. Certainly speaking for Oxfordshire County Council, at the time we were looking at adoption in the UK, the waiting list was four years for a new baby, and no one could join the waiting list unless both prospective parents would be still less than thirty-five years old by the time they were likely to reach the top of the list. This, of course, does raise very real problems for the childless couple. Very often by the time they have identified that their infertility is irreversible, they are already too old to join a waiting list for a new-born baby. There will be ample opportunity to ask questions about your own specific case and the atmosphere – although likely to be a little tense initially because the subject matter is so emotive – nonetheless, is generally friendly and helpful. You may even be offered a cup of tea!

2. PRELIMINARY INTERVIEW

A social worker will want to interview both partners together, either at home or possibly at their offices. This interview could take place prior to the information meeting or even in substitution for it, depending on how often the information meetings are held in your area. It has to be said that the speed of response you receive from the agency will be largely dependent on the 'value' of your offer. In other words, if you seem to be a good bet as prospective adoptive parents you are likely to get better and quicker attention!

3. PREPARATION GROUPS

Usually prior to the commencement of the home study process, you will be invited to attend a series of preparation group meetings – probably six to eight sessions over a period of about two months. Sometimes your performance at these group meetings may be used as a formal assessment but this will not happen blind. In other words if this is to be the procedure, you will be warned in advance. The main areas that will be explored during these preparation groups are as follows:

- The circumstances that lead couples to plan for adoption.

- The law.

- Implications for the child of separation and loss.

- Child development.

- Birth family issues such as maintaining links, telling children about their origins etc., etc.

- Management of behaviour in abused children.

- Behaviour management of children in general.

- Attitudes of prospective adopters to a range of different issues (see Chapter Three for this).

- Explaining the process – what is likely to happen next.

These meetings will take place in the format of small group discussions. Case studies will be used, as will videos, the whole object being to help prospective parents understand the complexity of the task ahead of them, and also to help them to assess their own ability to cope. It has to be said that there is a very high drop-out rate of prospective parents at these group sessions, which probably means that they are a good idea, since only the most committed remain. Having said that, I can't help feeling that there are a number of people who would probably make excellent adoptive parents who simply cannot bear these sort of meetings. Still, it is something you must be prepared to go through, if you seriously want to adopt.

4. THE HOME STUDY

The home study is a crucial document, for no other reason than that the quality of the future adopted child's life is dependent on its accuracy. To undertake a successful assessment there does need to be honest sharing of information between prospective adoptive parents and their social worker. It is terribly important that trust should develop and, of course, this may be difficult if you feel you need to be on your best behaviour. I think the best advice I can give is to say, 'relax'. To be honest my husband, Alan, and I were absolutely dreading our home study but in fact found it rather therapeutic. We all like talking about ourselves and if for one moment you can let your guard slip, you may well be quite surprised by what you have to say for yourself! A certain sort of person may consider the home study to be an invasion of privacy. While I have every sympathy, I do not think that the average agency will be well disposed towards this sort of attitude. You cannot expect to be entrusted with the life of a child unless you are prepared to disclose more or less everything there is to know about yourself, to your agency.

The home study has two main aspects to it:

(a) The social worker must evaluate what is being offered by the prospective adopters – their suitability, their strengths and their weaknesses.

(b) The social worker will also need to assess the adopters' capacity to develop and change through the assessment process, as they begin to understand more of their future role. This openness to learning and ability, to be able to operate in conjunction with someone else, is vital.

Supporting the home study, the following will also be required:

- A full medical report undertaken by a GP. This will be similar to medicals normally required for insurance purposes.

- Three references which can include one family member.

- Police checks on all members living in the household who are sixteen years or more.

- Record of individual interviews with both partners.

- A written contribution from both partners.

- A series of (probably between six and ten) interviews which will be rigorous and intimate with probing enquiries.

- Preparation of a book about the prospective parents to serve as an introduction for the child. This applies obviously for older children, rather than babies.

I thought it would be helpful to show you the layout of the form which social workers have to complete to form the basis of the home study. As you can see overleaf, it is a very comprehensive document but at least forewarned is forearmed.

During the course of the home study interview process there will be some very intimate questions which you may find difficult. For example:

- Applicants will be required to reflect upon their own childhood experiences. Their childhood will be discussed at some length, to see what sort of sense the applicant has made of it all – the idea being that this will help the social worker to grasp what sort of concepts of childhood the applicant will bring to the role of parenthood.

- Sexual relationships will be discussed and attitudes to sexuality will be explored.

- The link between fertility and sex will be discussed where the applicants have been unable to have children. For some couples the pleasurable aspects of sex will have been diminished during the desperate bid to conceive a child and they will be asked to consider the implications of this.

- In general terms applicants are asked to consider their own sense of sexuality and sexual boundaries to establish whether they are in a position to cope with children who have been sexually abused.

THE OFFICIAL ASSESSMENT

Form F — PART I — Information on prospective substitute parent(s) — Confidential

Please read notes for guidance before filling in the form and please ensure that all applicable sections are completed.

1. Agency details

- Name of Agency
- Address
- Tel. no.
- Name of social worker
- Name of senior social worker/team leader
- Tel. no.
- Name of link worker for inter-agency placement
- Tel. no.
- Date of completion of Part I
- Date of completion of Part II
- Updated

2. Details of applicant/s (state gender F/M)

	1st applicant	2nd applicant
Surname		
Previous name if applicable		
Forename(s)		
Known as		
Date of birth		
*Ethnic descent		
Language spoken at home		
Religion (please specify practising or nominal)		
Current/proposed hours of work		
Address		
Tel. no.		

Please attach recent photograph(s) of applicant(s)

3. Type of resource

PERMANENCE
- ☐ adoption
- ☐ adoption (with adoption allowance)
- ☐ long-term fostering
- ☐ other (eg residence order)

TIME LIMITED/TASK CENTRED
- ☐ Adolescents
- ☐ Bridging placement
- ☐ Emergency
- ☐ Observation & assessment
- ☐ Parent & child
- ☐ Other (please specify)
- ☐ Short term
- ☐ Respite care

*See paragraph on ethnicity in guidance notes.

Page 4:2

4. Matching considerations

This section is to be completed with the applicants after a full discussion of the issues (see Part II for greater detail)

Information on child/children you can consider

Age range (eg 9–12 years) _____

Number of children you can consider (if you can consider a single child or family group of two or three please circle 1, 2 or 3)

1   2   3   4   or more

Gender (please circle)   Male   Female   Either

If you can only consider a family group containing a particular gender, for example, 'including at least one boy', please state below

Religion: if there are any religions you CANNOT consider, please state below

Can you consider a child with a physical disability?	YES / NO
Can you consider a child with a mental disability?	YES / NO
Can you consider a child with a medical condition?	YES / NO
Can you consider a child who needs special education outside mainstream school?	YES / NO
Can you consider a child who is known to have been sexually abused?	YES / NO
Can you consider a child who has been physically abused?	YES / NO
Are there any restrictions on the type of contact with the birth family you could consider?	YES / NO

If the answer is YES to any of these questions, please expand further below and/or in Part II

Note: any child beyond babyhood will have a degree of emotional handicap

Please state any background factors you CANNOT consider (eg schizophrenia, child conceived of rape) below

Any specific comments you would like to add

5. Children in the household

Name	Gender	Date of birth	Ethnic descent	Type of school

Please state relationship to applicant/s (eg birth child, step-child, fostered, adopted, etc)

Page 4:3

THE OFFICIAL ASSESSMENT

Form F Part I   Confidential

6 Other children of the applicant/s (living elsewhere or deceased)

Name	Gender	Date of birth	Ethnic descent	Whereabouts (or date and cause of death)

State relationship to applicant/s

7 Other adult members of the household (including grown-up children living at home)

Name	Gender	Date of birth	Ethnic descent	Relationship (eg relative, lodger, friend)

8 Accommodation, neighbourhood, mobility

Type of accommodation: proposed sleeping arrangements for child. Description of neighbourhood: include ethnic mix and special amenities eg schools, medical resources, recreation facilities. If applicants plan to move, give details and any implications for a child placed. Indicate public transport facilities. Does the applicants have/use a car? Could the applicants travel for introductions? How would work and social commitments affect this? What support will the applicant/s need from the agency?

PAGE 44

Form F Part I   Confidential

9 Legal Information

State the court to which the adopter/s would apply

Is the applicant/s domiciled in the UK, Channel Islands or Isle of Man?   Yes / No

If no give domicile

Nationality: 1st applicant   2nd applicant

Can the applicant/s consider a child where legal situation is complex or delayed?   Yes / No
Please outline

Marital status

1st applicant _____ Gender _____
2nd applicant _____ Gender _____

If married to each other give place of marriage and date certificate or equivalent document seen

_____
_____

Length of marriage/partnership

Has either of the applicant/s had a previous marriage?   1st applicant: Yes / No   2nd applicant: Yes / No

If yes give details, how terminated and, if children involved, custody arrangement made. Specify documents seen.

10 Local authority enquiries (including police checks): as required under Adoption Agencies Regulations and Foster Placement Regulations. Please specify on whom checks were carried out and by which agency; include all adult members of the household and significant others.

1st applicant   2nd applicant   Other adults

State any comments from applicant re 10 above.

* Domicile is not the same as residence. The nearest definition is permanent home; a person may be resident for many years in another country without ceasing to be domiciled in the country s/he regards as 'home'. Legal advice should always be sought early in cases where there is any uncertainty.
† In the case of adoption the law only permits an adoption order in favour of one person or a married couple. Give more details in part II, number 8.

Page 45

Form F Part I — Confidential

11 Application, preparation groups, assessment

When was application first made?

State number of times applicant seen

For joint applicants state number of times seen

Together

Separately

1st applicant   2nd applicant

State the number and type of group meetings attended by the applicants; the ethnic mix of the group. Outline the specific subject areas covered; your assessment of the relevance of the group for the applicants and their contribution to the group. State the applicants' assessment of their development and the usefulness of what was offered. Identify any further areas of training needed and how these training needs will be met.

Where group preparation is not offered please state the type of preparation the applicants have received. Have they had the opportunity to learn about the needs/behaviours of children in care? Have they met experienced foster carers/adopters? What reading material have they had access to?

12 *Health (BAAF publishes standard medical forms for the examination of applicants)

Name, address and telephone number of family doctor(s)

Date of medical examination and comments of agency medical adviser (as recorded on Form Adult 1, and including significant comments from medical specialists).

1st applicant   2nd applicant

Medical reports should be updated every two years. The agency medical adviser (MA) will indicate whether this should be a further examination (Form Adult 1) or a report from medical records (Form Adult 2).

Update and MA's comments   (1st applicant)

Update and MA's comments   (2nd applicant)

Children of the household: any significant comments made by the doctor on their health or adjustment.

* See paragraph on confidentiality in guidance notes.

Page 48

Form F Part I — Confidential

Has any member of the household or extended family a physical, mental or emotional disability/difficulty (eg Alzheimer's disease, asthma, heart condition etc)? Include details of children with disabilities.

What is the applicants' attitude to health and ill-health/medical treatment generally? Are there any factors to consider in relation to medical treatment for a child please?

13 *Personal references (state whether referees have been interviewed)†

Indicate the relationship to the applicants and length of time they have known the applicants. Comment on their views of the applicants' ability to understand and relate to children; and on the applicants' ability to perform the tasks involved. Do they think the applicants will be able to ask for help/support? Do they have any reason to believe that the applicants might physically or sexually abuse a child?
How much weight would you give to the referees' assessment of the applicants?

Referee 1

Referee 2

* See paragraph on confidentiality in guidance notes.
† Adoption Agencies Regulations 1983 8(2)(e) require both referees to be personally interviewed.

© BAAF 1991   Page 49

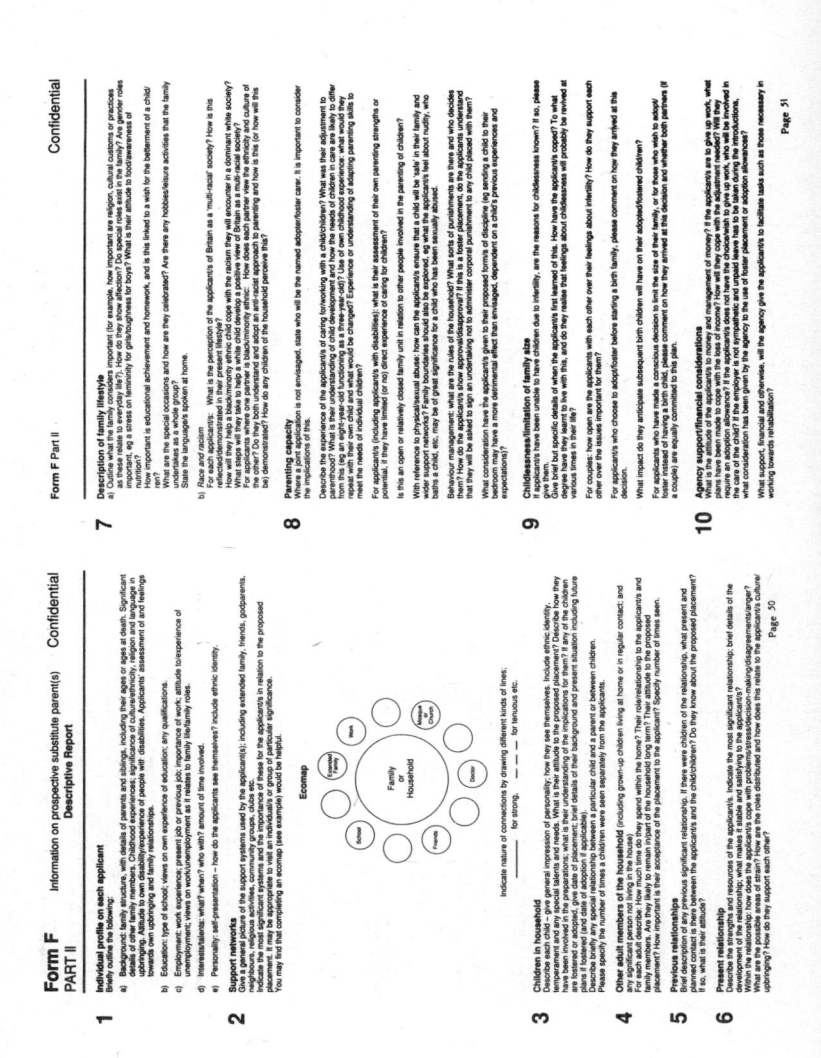

Form F   Information on prospective substitute parent(s)
PART II   Descriptive Report   Confidential

Briefly outline the following:

1   Individual profile on each applicant

a) Background; family structure, with details of parents and siblings, including their ages or ages at death. Significant details of other family members. Childhood experiences, significance of culture/ethnicity, religion and language in upbringing. Attitude to own disability/experience of people with disabilities. Applicants' assessment of and feelings about their own upbringing and family relationships.

b) Education; type of school, views on own experience of education, any qualifications.

c) Employment; work experience, present job or previous job, importance of work, attitude to/experience of unemployment; views on work/unemployment as it relates to family life/family roles.

d) Interests/talents: what? when? who with? amount of time involved.

e) Personality; self-presentation – how do the applicants see themselves? Include ethnic identity.

2   Support networks

Give a general picture of the support systems used by the applicant(s), including extended family, friends, godparents, neighbours, religious activities, community groups, clubs etc.
Indicate the significance and the importance of these for the applicants in relation to the proposed placement. It may be appropriate to visit an individual/s or group of particular significance.
You may find that completing an ecomap (see example) would be helpful.

Ecomap

(diagram: central circle labelled "Family or Household" surrounded by circles labelled "Work", "Extended Family", "School", "Church", "Friends", "Neighbours/Clubs")

Indicate nature of connections by drawing different kinds of lines:
——— for strong, – – – for tenuous etc.

3   Children in household

Describe each child – give general impression of personality; how they see themselves. Include ethnic identity, temperament and any special talents and needs. What is their attitude to the proposed placement? Describe how they have been involved in the preparation. What is their understanding of the implications for them? If any of the children are fostered or adopted, give date of placement; brief details of their background and present situation including future plans if fostered (and date of adoption if applicable).
Describe briefly any significant relationship between a particular child and a parent or between children.
Please specify the number of times 2 children were seen separately from the applicants.

4   Other adult members of the household (including grown-up children living at home or in regular contact; and any significant person not living in the house)

For each adult describe: How much time they spend within the home? Their role/relationship to the applicants and family members. Are they likely to remain impact of the household long term? Their attitude to the proposed placement? How important is their acceptance of the placement to the applicants? Specify number of times seen.

5   Previous relationships

Brief description of any previous significant relationship, if there were children of the relationship, what present and planned contact is there between the applicants and the children/ren? Do they know about the proposed placement?

6   Present relationship

Describe the strengths and resources of the applicant/s. Indicate the most significant relationship; brief details of the development of the relationship, what makes it stable and satisfying to the applicants?
Within the relationship: how does the applicants cope with problems/stress/decision-making/disagreements/anger?
What are the possible areas of strain? How are the roles distributed and how does this relate to the applicants' culture/upbringing? How do they support each other?

Page 50

Form F Part II   Confidential

7   Description of family lifestyle

a) Outline what the family considers important (for example, how important is family cohesion, are these views related to everyday life?). How do they show affection? Do special roles exist in the family? Are gender roles important, eg a stress on femininity for girls/toughness for boys? What is their attitude to food/awareness of nutrition?
How important is educational achievement and homework, and is this linked to a wish for the betterment of a child/ren?
What are the special occasions and how are they celebrated? Are there any hobbies/leisure activities that the family undertakes as a whole group?
State the languages spoken at home.

b) Race and racism
For each applicant: What is the perception of the applicant/s of Britain as a 'multi-racial' society? How is the education/demonstrated in their present lifestyle?
How will they help a black/minority ethnic child cope with the racism they will encounter in a dominant white society? What stage will they take to help a white child develop a positive view of Britain as a multi-racial society?
For applicants where one partner is black/minority ethnic. How does each partner view the ethnicity and culture of the other? Do they both understand and adopt an anti-racist approach to parenting and how are the family be demonstrated? How do any children of the household perceive this?

8   Parenting capacity

Where a joint application is not envisaged, state who will be the named adopter/foster carer. It is important to consider the implications of this.

Describe the experience of the applicants of caring for/working with a child/children? What was their adjustment to parenthood? What is their understanding of child development and how the needs of children in care are likely to differ from this (eg an eight-year-old functioning as a three-year-old)? Use of own childhood experience; what would they repeat with their own child and what would be changed? Experience or understanding of adapting parenting skills to meet the needs of individual children?

For applicants (including applicants with disabilities): what is their assessment of their own parenting strengths or potential, if they have limited (or no) direct experience of caring for children?

Is this an open or relatively closed family unit in relation to other people involved in the parenting of children?

With reference to physical/sexual abuse: how can the applicants ensure that a child will be 'safe' in their family and wider support networks? Family boundaries should also be explored, eg what the applicants feel about nudity, who baths a child, etc, may be of great significance for a child who has been sexually abused.

Behaviour management: what are the views of the household? What sorts of punishments are there and who decides them? Would they feel able to follow the foster placement, do the applicants understand that they can be asked to sign an undertaking not to administer corporal punishment to any child placed with them?

What consideration have the applicants given to their proposed forms of discipline (eg sending a child to their bedroom) may have a more detrimental effect than envisaged, dependent on a child's previous experiences and expectations)?

9   Childlessness/limitation of family size

If applicants have been unable to have children due to infertility, are the reasons for childlessness known? If so, please give them.

Give brief but specific details of when the applicants first learned of the infertility. How have the applicants coped? To what degree have they wanted to live with this, and do they realise that feelings about childlessness will probably be revived at various times in their life?

For couples: how open are the applicants with each other over their feelings about infertility? How do they support each other over the issues important to them?

For applicants who choose to adopt/foster before starting a birth family, please comment on how they arrived at this decision.

What impact do they anticipate subsequent birth children will have on their adopted/fostered children?

For applicants who have made a conscious decision to limit the size of their family, for the use of adoption/foster instead of having a birth child, please comment on how they arrived at the decision and whether both partners (if a couple) are equally committed to this plan.

10   Agency support/financial considerations

What is the attitude of the applicants to money and management of money? If the applicants are to give up work, what plans have been made to cope with the loss of income? How will they cope with the adjustment needed? Will they require an education allowance? If the applicants do not intend to take time off to settle a child, who will be involved in the care of the child? If the employer is not sympathetic and could leave has to be taken during the introductions, what consideration has been given by the agency to the use of foster placement or adoption allowances?

What support, financial and otherwise, will the agency give the applicants to facilitate tasks such as those necessary in working towards rehabilitation?

Page 51

Form F Part II — Confidential

11. Placement and post-placement considerations

a) Background factors What is the understanding of the applicants of the social pressures contributing to children being 'looked after/accommodated'? What is their appreciation of the effects of separation/loss/lack of attachments upon children? What are their feelings about heredity? What is their attitude to mental ill-health? Do they have an understanding of social pressures contributing to many? Would they accept a child where little is known about the father and/or the mother?

What is their attitude to telling/sharing information with an adopted child about their origins? Is there any information the applicants find difficult to tell and what would be the agency's role in this case?

b) Child as she/he is What is the understanding of the applicants of possible areas of disturbance? Do they appreciate that poor self-esteem might be at the base of many behavioural problems? What sorts of behaviours would they feel most confident in dealing with and which might they find difficult. For example delayed or excessive affection, sleep problems, under-eating, over-eating, soiling, acting out, attention seeking, rivalry, bullying, bed wetting, stealing, aggression, destructiveness, cruelty.

Identity problems: does the applicant understand that some black/minority ethnic children, including those of mixed parentage (on entry or as a consequence of being 'looked after/accommodated'), will have a negative black self-image, and some will wish to deny their black identity altogether? How will the applicant's envisage tackling this predicament? What consideration has the agency given to supporting a black/minority ethnic applicant in this situation?

Sexual abuse: can the applicant's cope with a child who has been sexually abused? Is there any overtly sexual behaviour the applicant's could not deal with? Would they be able to cope with a child born of an incestuous relationship?

Puberty/adolescence: what is the attitude of the applicants to emerging sexuality/sexual development/sexual experimentation? How do they view sexual education? What is their attitude to some group pressures: mood swings/ regression? smoking? drug experimentation? alcohol abuse? and independence generally? How would they support a child who was lesbian or gay? What are the potential areas of difficulty they envisage for themselves?

Medical problems: indicate the specific conditions they could consider. Would the applicant's be able to care for a child at risk of HIV infection/AIDS and what is their understanding of and capacity to deal with the associated issues, eg the need for confidentiality? Would they have the ability to help a child with the loss of a birth parents and the uncertainty of their own circumstances? What medical resources are available locally?

Physical disabilities/learning difficulties: can the applicants consider a child with a physical disability? If so, indicate what specific needs they feel able to meet. In the case of a severely disabled child, is their accommodation suitable or will they require help to adapt it appropriately? What are the local resources for therapy and respite care? How would the applicants cope with a child with learning difficulties? Indicate whether they would consider (a) mild, moderate or severe difficulties, (b) a child who would need to attend a special school; or (c) a child who would require remedial help in mainstream school only. What is the attitude of the applicants towards a young adult's transition to independent living? Would the applicants, in that situation, have the understanding needs of a learning person with physical/learning disabilities/difficulties? Do the applicants have any special skills, experience of local facilities, etc to offer?

For baby adopters: are they prepared for the possibility of a baby being placed with them directly from the hospital? What is their attitude to this and their understanding of the implications?

c) Contact with birth family/people from the child's past. How far are the applicant's prepared to maintain a child's links with their birth family, eg through the exchange of photos and letters both on a short term and long term basis? What face-to-face contact with family and significant others are the applicants prepared for, and how often and with what frequency?

Are the applicants prepared to:

a) Work with the parents and the agency towards rehabilitation or another placement?
b) Help a child in a positive way to make sense of her/his experience with her/his birth parents?
c) Understand why a child may be distressed after visits?
d) Be willing and/or able to offer visiting parents meals, overnight accommodation regularly/occasionally?
e) Sensitively deal with challenging behaviour from a parents or relative/s?

12. Post adoption

What particular issues/problems do the applicants envisage for themselves and their children during adolescence/ when adoption becomes real for the children? Will the applicants be able to support the young person in their search for information (access to birth records)? What consideration has been given to the possibility of: (a) disruption and the after-effects on the applicants; (b) breakdown of the relationship and the implications for continued parenting? What post-adoption support is the agency able to offer and are the applicants aware of this and other resources which they can call on?

For further guidance on assessment, refer to paragraphs 3.12 to 3.32 in The Children Act 1989 Guidance and Regulations, Volume 3: Family Placements, HMSO 1991.

© BAAF 1991

Page 52

Social worker's assessment
Please attach this to the back page of the descriptive report

Comment on the expressed motivation of the applicants to adopt/foster.
What skills do you think they have in relating to and working with a child/children? What sort of children would the applicants probably do best with? How did they impress you at first and on closer acquaintance? How will these work with the agency, with other officials, with birth parents and with the child? Comment on the strengths and resources of the applicants and on the areas where they may experience difficulty. If there is any point of disagreement between you and them, it is important to record it here. Please state your recommendation.

For black/minority ethnic applicant's state the type and amount of involvement of black/minority ethnic professionals in this assessment.

Applicant's signatures

1st applicant _____ Date _____

2nd applicant _____ Date _____

Social worker's signature _____ Date _____

Team leader's signature _____ Date _____

Agency approval _____ Date _____
(please specify age range, numbers etc)

© BAAF 1991

Page 53

These are fairly weighty issues and daunting subjects to discuss, particularly with someone who is a virtual stranger to you. Even in front of your partner you may find these subjects difficult. You may feel that you have an excellent understanding of one another and each other's attitudes, but you may not wish to discuss them, particularly with someone else. I am very sympathetic to this view – the British, in particular, are notoriously bad at talking about these sort of issues. Nonetheless, one can see from the agencies' point of view that it is desperately important that a potential adoptive parent is thoroughly investigated. It is not fair. All sorts of potentially unsuitable people create babies – sometimes parenthood is the making of them, sometimes they wreck their children's lives ... yet a natural parent has to ask no one before assuming the role. It is very understandable to feel aggrieved at having to go through such a rigorous process. You are probably confident that you would make an ideal adoptive parent – you have all the love in the world to give – security and comfort. Why is it necessary for you to go through this ordeal? I can only bring you back to the first sentence of this book, 'Adoption means caring for someone else's child.' It is a big responsibility.

Once the home study is completed, you will be shown what has been said about you which can often be quite illuminating. The only parts which are excluded from the home study are the personal references and the police reports. The whole procedure should take between four and six months, or in certain circumstances it can be speeded up a little if a particular child is in desperate need. I think it is helpful if you can try and look at the home study procedure as a unique experience, and a positive one. It can be very revealing, not only to yourself but also to your partner. It is not supposed to be a particularly comfortable experience and sometimes may be very demanding, but it is a worthwhile exercise and, hopefully, you can view it as such.

5. THE ADOPTION PANEL

Once your application to adopt is completed, it will be put before an adoption panel. The adoption panel is comprised of a maximum of ten people. It will include a medical adviser, a local counsellor and at least two independent people who are specifically child orientated – ie., adoptive parents, teachers etc., etc. The chairman is often a member of the agency, but not always so. The adoption panel have three quite specific tasks:

(a) To decide on a plan – ie. whether to free the child for adoption.

(b) To approve the adoptive parents.

(c) To approve the link between child and prospective adoptive parents.

You will not be present at the panel meeting. Your report would be presented by the social worker who prepared your home study. Approval, when it is given, will be in relation to the specific number of children you will be allowed to adopt, the sex, the age range and the nature of the child. Sometimes, because the adopters are already seeking adoption of a specific child, approval will be given for the child only. In other words, sometimes the cart comes before the horse – the child is identified before the assessment begins. This is particularly true of overseas adoption, of which there will be full details in Chapter Fourteen. If approval is given for a non-specific child, then clearly it will be necessary to go before the panel again when you have found a child so that the linking can be approved. The adoption panel's decision is final – there can be no appeal. The good news is that you should have their verdict verbally within a few days.

6. FINDING A CHILD

Once the adoption panel have approved your case, the timescale for a placement depends enormously on the kind of child you are hoping to adopt, and, of course, the area in which you live. In other words, availability is the criteria. If you have been approved for a sibling group, a disabled child or an older child, then your chances of a fairly speedy placement are high. If on the other hand you are quite specifically looking for a pre-school child without serious disability, it could be a long wait. It sounds dreadful expressed in these terms, as if one is talking about mail-order shopping. Perhaps it is here that it might be most appropriate to re-emphasize the difference between adoption and conceiving a child of your own. The birth of a child is surrounded by such emotive images as flouncy, lacy shawls, Moses baskets, soft woolly teddy bears, gentle smiles and love – a perfect baby, cooing in a perfect world. Oh, that it were so! Adopting a child is no substitute for this image of parenthood. It is a tough job and because it is a tough job, you are rigorously interviewed and assessed to see whether you are tough enough to cope. Many of the children available for adoption have known nothing but unkindness and insecurity in their lives and, of course, they have been affected – *seriously affected*. You are not going to find the perfect child, but you might well fall in love with a gutsy little character for whom you may be the first decent thing that has ever happened in his life.

One way in which you can help yourself is to join PPIAS – Parent to Parent Information on Adoption Services. PPIAS produce a quarterly newsletter, quite literally advertising children who are available for adoption. This enables you to contact any local authority in the country concerning a specific child. They also provide an information pack and a book list. The annual subscription is £8 and for details you should write to Philly Morrall at the address shown in the back of this book. PPIAS include all sorts of children in their newsletters, of all ethnic origins, ages, some with disabilities and some sibling groups. Reading one of their newsletters, if nothing else, will make you realize the crying need to find permanent homes for these children.

It would also be sensible to contact BAAF (The British Agency for Adoption and Fostering). BAAF is a charity and professional association aimed at those working in the child care field. It seeks to promote high standards of practice in adoption, fostering and child care, and to influence policy and practice by, for example, giving evidence and advice to government departments. BAAF also provides training and consultancy, and assists the public by giving advice and information. BAAF also operates a linking system, putting one agency in touch with another, in the search for suitable families. Fees are paid by the agency with whom the child is placed, to the agency who represent the adopters. As a prospective adopter, you can approach BAAF even before you have approached an agency, and BAAF will in turn notify the appropriate agency of your interest. However, I would suggest that your best approach is direct to an agency, as it is important to make personal contact when making your selection. The BAAF publication *Adopting a Child* is an invaluable source of information, and includes names and addresses of all adoption agencies in the UK, plus advice and details on the issues associated with adoption. This could well be a starting point for you.

Most agencies advertise quite extensively the children who are available in their area:

- Through newspapers, local and national.

- Radio or TV, particularly the 'Find a Family' campaign which usually co-incides with Foster Care Week.

- Through adoption shops. Some agencies use shop fronts to feature individual children – sometimes in a fairly anonymous way but sometimes identifying children very clearly.

Whether you are looking at an agency advertisement or one in the PPIAS newsletter, you will find that children are described in terms which make them appear *relatively* unproblematic. Of course they look enchanting and endearing, because they are children and that is how children look. However it is very important not to be naïve. These photographs and descriptions of the children involved, only tell part of the truth. Social workers, unlike dubious estate agents and used-car salesmen, do not deliberately seek to mislead the 'potential customer'. They have to be sensitive to the children and to the children's families, and there is no point in painting an inaccurate picture which will only lead to a placement breaking down. However, they are often constrained by legal requirements as to what they are able to say in an advertisement, so some censorship is legitimately necessary. In addition, it is true to say that social workers, like estate agents, have a 'commodity to promote' and their initial intention is to attract as much interest in the children they are advertising, as possible. So be prepared to read between the lines of any advertisement and recognize that if you proceed with an inquiry, you are going to hear and read much less glowing descriptions of the child in the fullness of time. Never be reluctant to ask questions about the child. There is so much at stake, emotionally and practically for all concerned. Social workers are very often under huge pressure and may well not be able to remember what they said to one prospective parent or to another. They may not deliberately withhold information, but they may forget to share it, so keep worrying at the problem until you find you have all the information you need, about a specific child.

As you are given more details, you are likely to feel a range of emotions – shock, anger, frustration, sadness … and these emotions will become increasingly familiar as you learn about the children who need substitute families, and the process which seeks to bring them together with new families. Balancing the needs of everyone in the adoption triangle is nothing short of a nightmare!

Certainly, unless you are waiting for a newborn baby, I do think you need to create your own luck. In other words do not rely solely on your agency to find a child for you. Of course a lot depends on your value to the agency as to what sort of treatment you get (as already described), but it is important to keep a sense of your own self worth. Certainly once you are approved, you become a more valuable commodity, and while you must recognize that waiting periods may be quite long, do not be complacent. If we equate for a moment, giving birth to a child with adoption, the home study, if you like, is the conception. However, unlike giving birth, where one merely has to conceive and hang around for nine months, adoption is not that simple. Once conception has taken place, you can only move on to the next stage by keeping up the pressure and not being afraid to hassle!

So there you have it, the process of approval in a nutshell. If I have made it sound simple, I am sorry, for it is not. There will be all sorts of frustrating delays, there will be times when you will be quite sure that you are doing the wrong thing. Yet against this there will be other times of enormous elation as the prospect of parenthood begins to look like a real possibility. As I have said, it is a rigorous process – in many respects I think too rigorous – but then mistakes must not be made. In some areas the process is far from efficient and the degree of enthusiasm and speed with which your social worker deals with your application, will depend hugely on the need within the area and your ability to fill it. You must keep clearly in the front of your mind that it is *not* your social worker's job to find you a child and fulfil your desire for parenthood. The social worker's job is to find suitable families for the child in care. Be patient.

5

Children available for adoption

I hope in the course of this book I have already emphasized the harsh realities associated with most children who are available for adoption. These are not bad children, or in may instances, even truly problem children, but almost certainly any child available for adoption will have suffered a major separation experience. Some, of course, will have had no love or security in their whole lives. Some will have had it and lost it. Some will have put blind faith in a parent again and again, only to have been let down again and again. Some will be confused, some will have simply switched off. Children have a tendency to blame themselves when things go wrong; when their parents' marriage breaks down, when they are neglected, even abused. They take on responsibility for what has happened, heightening their sense of failure and guilt.

When a child has been in and out of care and has lived with a number of different foster families, the damage sustained is enormous. Across the country, social workers have been amazed at the speed with which the children who were adopted from Romanian orphanages have adjusted to life with their new adoptive parents. Few show any signs of the ordeal they have been through, which is hard to understand on the face of it when one considers the degree of malnutrition and neglect they suffered. The conclusion reached is that at least their life was stable – their mothers left them in orphanages where they simply vegetated, with barely enough food to keep them alive and the minimum of attention to do the same – they simply went into a state of limbo. Once they were given love, attention, care and good food, it was like the switching on of a light bulb, and in a way the long-term damage they sustained is probably less than a child who has known three different foster families and has experienced four attempts to rehabilitate him with his mother. So, the message here is that the children available for adoption will almost certainly have been through a great deal of trauma and stress in their lives and the problems associated with this should not be underestimated.

Because of this, agencies find that smaller children are far easier to place. Not only do they tie in more closely with the childless couples' image of parenthood, but they also bring with them less 'baggage'. Whatever a tiny, pre-school child has been through, there is the very genuine and realistic belief that the child's problems can be ironed out in the long term. With an older child, there may be grounds for saying that the damage sustained is so severe, the child may never fully recover. This is a very depressing notion, but it is understandable that prospective adoptive parents do feel very daunted at the prospect of caring for an older child. Officially any child can be adopted up to the age of eighteen, but in practice few children past the age of fourteen are adopted.

As I have already explained, there is a very long waiting

list for newborn babies and traditionally both parents have had to be under the age of thirty-five or thereabouts at the time of reaching the top of that list. Similarly, if you can only undertake the adoption of a pre-school child with no handicaps or special needs, again the wait may be a long one. There are, however, five basic categories of children who are considered hard to place and in theory these children should be more readily available for adoption. Let us look at these categories in more detail.

1. MIXED PARENTAGE

A child of mixed parentage, ie. black and white, is perceived as black. Initially social workers will be looking to place that child with either, ideally, a mixed-race family or, if not, then a black family. There has been much controversy over this and rightly so. Because a child is perceived black, it is surely not right to ignore the white element of the child's culture. In addition, as I have previously indicated, the child of a mixed-race relationship usually has a white mother and a black father. If the child was living with just one of the natural parents, which in most cases is more likely to be the mother, then the child would have been brought up in a white environment anyway. Some local authorities are absolutely adamant that these children either have to go to a mixed-race family or if none is available, they have to stay in children's homes or foster care for their entire childhood. Other authorities take a less bigoted view – if no black or mixed-race families are available in their area then they will consider a white family, particularly a white family who can demonstrate that they either have black friends or some association with black culture.

2. PSYCHIATRIC ILLNESS

Very often children come into care as a result of their parents having a psychiatric problem, which is likely to be visited on the child. Perhaps the most common of these is schizophrenia. At the time a placement is being sought for the child, he or she may be unaffected, but if the prognosis remains uncertain, this naturally makes the child difficult to place. Sometimes the future is known – the child may already be affected and the course of the illness fairly predictable. Either way, these children do need special help. Many agencies feel would-be adoptive parents are better equipped if they have had some specific experience – either of the type of illness itself or, at the very least, of handling children. If you feel that this is an area where you can help, it will be possible to obtain plenty of factual information and counselling both prior to and during the placement of the child. You should discuss this with your Social Services.

3. SIBLING GROUPS

Sibling groups are harder to place, for practical reasons and because obviously taking on a number of children is a very daunting prospect. Where there are more than two children involved, it is highly likely that the children will come from different foster homes, and although they are siblings, they may have spent very little time together. This means that the children not only have to adjust to living with you, but adjust to living with each other. There is a considerable degree of practical help in terms of both money and equipment available to parents who take on sibling groups. More of this in Chapter Six. I think it is important to emphasize that practical obstacles are relatively easy to overcome. It is the problem associated with trying to make a home for several children at once, all likely to be very demanding, which is going to prove the greatest hurdle. The more children involved, the more versatile you will have to be. Nonetheless, if you and your partner feel this is something with which you could cope it is a wonderful thing to do, to bring a family together and give them a home under one roof, perhaps for the first time in their lives. One of the many problems facing adopted children is their sense of identity and the need to make contact with their origins. In a sibling group this is much less of a problem, they all have each other.

4. THE DISABLED CHILD

Mercifully, due to pregnancy testing, the number of severely disabled children born has been greatly reduced. However, when mothers do not attend ante-natal clinics, disabilities still occur. These of course can range from relatively minor disabling features to the grossly disabled child who may only have a short life span. Sometimes parents specialize in children with a specific disability, as with the inspiring story of May and David.

> *May rang me just over two years ago to ask for help in trying to bring a little girl out of a Romanian orphanage, who was suffering from hydrocephalus. Apparently the child, about nine months old, was in extreme distress and needed an operation to put in a shunt to relieve the pressure on her brain. Neither the Department of Health in the UK, nor the Romanian judicial system were being at all helpful.*

During the course of the next two or three months, while we helped May with her legal battles to bring little Alexandra home to England, I learnt more about her extraordinary story. She and David have two sons, now grown up. When the youngest boy was six they had another child, a little girl who was born with hydrocephalus. With much love and careful nursing, she lived to be six years old, and died at home, peacefully, surrounded by her family. David and May felt the loss keenly. They had never had any difficulty in accepting their daughter's condition and had made sure her short life was as happy and as comfortable as possible. A few weeks after her death, they went back to the childrens' hospital ward where the little girl had spent so many weeks during her life, to thank the staff. There was another little girl lying in a cot with a condition identical to their daughter's but with one big difference. The child had been abandoned at birth by parents who felt they simply could not cope with the extent of her disability.

David and May had a real problem with their Social Services. The moment they saw the child it became clear to them that here was something that they could do to help, something that would make sense of their daughter's death. The Social Services were not impressed. As they saw it, May was simply trying to cope with her grief by transferring her love to another child. David and May persisted. They were helped by the fact that there was no other family in the region prepared to take responsibility for the child, who technically no longer needed to be hospitalized. In the end they won, and so began fifteen years of caring for children with hydrocephalus. We managed to get little Alexandra home four months after May had first telephoned me. She died a year later, but in that time she had experienced all the love and care that is every child's right. She was the fifth child to have died in May and David's arms but theirs is not a story of defeat, but one of triumph.

Certainly if you feel that you can cope with caring for a disabled child, perhaps because you already have some experience of a particular disability, or because you are in a caring profession, then do follow your instincts – there are many children available.

5. AIDS BABIES

Increasingly, particularly in certain areas of the country, babies are coming into care who are HIV positive. This may be because their parents already have full blown AIDS, or have died of AIDS, or because the parents cannot cope with looking after a baby – perhaps they are drug addicts. As we are all painfully aware, there is no cure for AIDS and sooner or later a baby who is HIV positive is likely to develop the full-blown illness. (Occasionally, very young children who test HIV positive as a result of contracting the disease in the womb, appear to lose their HIV status. At the moment, their futures remain uncertain.)

The practical problems of caring for a child who is HIV positive, are extremely simple. By following a few basic rules of hygiene and common sense, there is no question of you or your family becoming affected. The main problems are emotional, rather than practical.

(a) The effect of bereavement on you and your family. Essentially you will be adopting a child over whom hangs a death sentence. You will learn to love the child, you will put to the back of your mind that the child may not always be with you, and the more deeply your relationship grows, the harder it will be to face up to what the future is almost certain to bring. Maybe a cure will be found in time, maybe the blood tests were wrong ... you will look in moments of stress for avenues which will ensure that you can keep your child with you forever, but the reality is different and you will know it deep down, however much you try to fool yourself. For this reason you need to be very sure that you can cope with the implications emotionally and of course, there may not just be you and your partner to consider. If you have other children, you need to look at how you feel they would cope with such a close bereavement, and whether it is fair to inflict one on them.

(b) The second main problem is other people's reactions. It does not feel right or fair to keep the knowledge of your child's condition to yourself, but the moment it becomes known, there will be problems for your child, and for your family as a whole. Many parents will not want their children to play with your child; you may have great difficulty finding a school which will take the child and you are likely to find your whole family being ostracized by certain members of society. Despite all the publicity surrounding AIDS, there are people who still believe that you can catch the disease from sharing a coffee cup. Certainly taking on an AIDS baby will be a great leveller – you will very soon find out who your true friends are, but you should not underestimate the degree of prejudice you are likely to encounter.

Up to a point what I have said about AIDS applies to Hepatitis B. Children who are carriers of Hepatitis B are thankfully unlikely to die. It is possible that they may develop liver cancer or liver complications in later life which could prove fatal, but increasingly, control of Hepatitis B is improving and in many instances children lose their Hepatitis B carrying status as the years go by. Nonetheless, if you take on a child who is a Hepatitis B carrier, you are likely to encounter the same sort of prejudices as is the case with AIDS.

6. CHILDREN IN DOUBLE FIGURES

In theory a child can be adopted at any time up to the age of eighteen, though in practice this rarely happens over the age of fourteen. Indeed, once a child is in double figures there are far fewer prospective adoptive parents who are likely to be interested in adoption, and in any event adoption is often not appropriate for the older child. Teenagers who have lead entirely happy, secure lives can be monstrous. A child who has suffered a great deal can be very hard work, if not impossible to handle during adolescence.

Of course, it is very sad to miss out on the bulk of your son or daughter's childhood, particularly when that childhood has been unhappy. Nonetheless, a child in double figures is still right at the very beginning of his or her life. To be able to give that life some sort of focus, security and love is the most marvellous thing. Maybe you cannot heal all the hurts as you could have done with a much younger child, but you still can offer a framework, a safety net, *you can still be that child's family*. Of course, in every society there are some parents and children who virtually part company the moment the child leaves school which is very sad. However, for most loving families, even though they will inevitably have their quarrels and dramas, children and parents stay close. When my grandmother died, her three children sobbed their way through her funeral and all of them were drawing their old age pension! They may have been in their late sixties, but they still loved their Mum, saw her regularly, and their grief was a very real thing.

So, although a fifteen-year-old has said goodbye to real childhood, he still needs someone in his life. Maybe you and your partner are people who could provide a home for this sort of child. The need is so great and there are relatively few parents who are prepared to take on older children.

These then are the groupings in which the most number of children are available for adoption. A daunting selection, yes, but this is certainly the area where the needs are greatest.

Social status of child

This is a slightly awkward subject to raise but, nonetheless, I think it needs airing. Not all, but most, children in care come from socially deprived families. By contrast most prospective adoptive parents tend to come from a more middle-class background. The children who end up in care are so often the victims of their parents' own poor parenting – lack of money, poor housing and unemployment puts a terrible strain on people. Life ceases to have a purpose for the parents and inevitably in their frustration, children get hurt.

The social differences between adopted children and their parents may not be a problem provided that the parents handle it sensitively. If you are able to offer a child from a very deprived background his own bedroom, bicycle, holidays in the sun, possibly even a private education, it must be done sensitively. It is vital to stress to the child that this change of lifestyle is not better necessarily but different and that it is not his birth parents' fault that they could not offer the same. You must be very careful not to give the child the impression that money solves everything.

The other major problem, of course, is associated with the adoptive parents' likely reaction to the child's behaviour. They may find it extremely shocking, both in terms of language, habits and cleanliness, and this may make it very difficult to see how everyone can ever shake down into a family. What is important is to try and find common threads. Maybe the adoptive father and child have a mutual passion for football or motorbikes. Maybe mother and daughter are mad about animals. If there is the common ground of interests between you, then the social differences become a great deal less important and gradually will be ironed out. Common ground is all about liking the same sort of things and enjoying doing the same sort of activities. If you have this in common with your child, then the rest will follow.

In conclusion, therefore, the type of child who is available to you for adoption depends to a large extent on your circumstances, your age, your experience, your marital status, your general attitude towards parenthood and, of course, the amount of time you have available to devote to the role. As a general rule of thumb, it would be true to say that there is a fairly substantial number of hard-to-place children available for adoption and relatively few whose problems are neither severe nor long term. If you do not feel you can cope with the problems you are likely to confront in adopting a child from the UK, then you could consider adopting a very small child from abroad who although he/she may have suffered a higher degree of deprivation, may not be so emotionally scarred. More of this in Chapter Fourteen. Suffice to say here, though, that if you can be open-minded, you might surprise yourself with your ability to cope with all sorts of problems, given the right degree of encouragement and preparation.

6

The financial aspects of adoption

Adopting a child within the UK is not an expensive business in so far as the acquisition of the child is concerned. If you are adopting from abroad, however, it is a completely different situation and may involve many thousands of pounds. Here in the UK you can equate adopting a child in financial terms to giving birth. The State picks up the tab for most of the expenses. The actual legal process of adoption will not require you to have a lawyer, provided the case is straightforward and so there will be no legal costs involved. If the case is contested, then it is possible that the agency may direct you towards a specific lawyer to represent you, but in any event the agency will settle the lawyer's costs at the end of the case. A contested case is unusual, mostly because children have been cleared for adoption before prospective adoptive parents are even aware of their existence. A contested case is most likely to occur in the case of foster parents who seek the adoption of their foster child. It may be that a child has lived with a family for some years and both the family and social worker feel that it is in the best interests of the child for it to be formally adopted into the family. At this point the child's birth parents may well contest such a move, even though they have expressed little or no interest in the child up to this point. In most adoptions, however, the legalities surrounding the actual making of an adoption order should be very straightforward.

In general terms, therefore, apart from the time you and your partner may have had to take off work in order to be with the child or attend meetings, there should be no heavy financial burden until the child comes to live with you. Once he or she does, however, the child is your child and your responsibility in every degree, including financially. There are various financial aspects of which you should be aware.

1. CHILD ALLOWANCE

From the moment the child comes to live with you, and assuming the plan is clearly for adoption, you are eligible for Child Allowance, even if the adoption process has not been completed. The only circumstances in which this would not apply would be if you were fostering the child and receiving a fostering allowance. If this was the case, you would not be granted child allowance as well.

2. MATERNITY ALLOWANCE AND LEAVE

Adoptive parents have no rights to either maternity allowance or maternity leave whether the child that comes into their care is a brand new baby or an older child. I consider this to be an appalling oversight but apparently the

Government is not planning to do anything about it. Of course, some companies can be very understanding and may be only too pleased to award you your full compliment of both allowance and leave, even though they are not legally bound to do so. But many employers, particularly in today's difficult economic climate, may be much relieved not to have to take on this responsibility. If this is the case, there is absolutely nothing you can do about it. Jean's story proves the point.

> *I used to work in a privately owned supermarket, in a small town in Gloucestershire. I worked as secretary to the Managing Director but was always prepared to do anything – stack shelves, go on the till, anything if we were short staffed. My boss seemed very appreciative. I was relatively well paid but I jolly well worked for it. During the whole time I was employed, both my boss and his wife knew that Tom, my husband, and I were desperately trying to have a baby. When it became clear that we would never be able to conceive a child they were very sympathetic.*
>
> *After a fairly lengthy period of grieving, Tom and I pulled ourselves together and decided we would try and adopt. We were very lucky. Within a year of our decision, our local Social Services put us in touch with a little boy called Neil, who was six. His history was very sad. His mother was dead, he had been abused by an uncle and moved from one relation to another before being taken into care permanently at four. Tom and I fell for him immediately we met, there were no doubts at all and Neil seemed to feel the same way, too. Our social worker warned us, though, that we were in for a rough ride. She said there would be a honeymoon period and then Neil would start to test us. Apparently, in her view,*

he had never really formed a proper emotional attachment with anyone in his life and he was going to put us through a very hard time before he would allow himself to love us.

I explained all this to my boss and his wife, expecting them to be really thrilled for us. Neil was due to come and live with us on 7th July and I asked if I could have the whole of July and August off work and aimed to be back by mid-September.

I could not believe it when they said no. I tried again, explaining that I was not asking to be paid, just to have the time off and for them to hold my job open. 'If he is six he will be at school,' my boss's wife said. I explained, as patiently as I could, that the time I was asking for represented the whole of the summer holidays. Naturally, Tom and I wanted to spend as much time as we possibly could with Neil during this period in the hopes that we could overcome many of our difficulties by the time he had to face a new school in the autumn. My boss was unimpressed. He simply said that our busiest time was during the summer holidays – which of course was true being in a tourist area – and that he was not prepared to hold the job open for me.

So I did the only thing I could in the circumstances, and resigned. I could not believe that they had done this to me after twelve years of working for them. Nor could I believe that there was nothing I could do to force them to reconsider their decision.

Tom was luckier. He, admittedly, was only asking for a month off and his firm readily agreed to this and even continued to pay his salary. As Tom is the main earner in our family, this was a blessing and of course we were very grateful.

We had a very hard summer with Neil. It was lovely

in parts, other times heartbreaking and exhausting but I do not regret for a single moment the decision I took to take time off work. By the time I delivered our little boy to the school gates in September, we had made it, we were a family. Although, of course, there has been the odd hiccup since, that time spent exclusively with Neil was absolutely vital to our future together. I have been very lucky with my job. I am now working in the office of a large comprehensive school, just up the road from Neil's school. The hours fit in with his and I have already discussed with them the possibility of our adopting another child. Of course we will try to coincide with the school holidays but that may not happen. The headmaster has already promised me whatever time off I need to settle in a new one, if we are lucky enough to be able to adopt a second child. I still feel, though, that there is something wrong with the law that allowed my former boss to get away with treating me as he did.

3. ADOPTION ALLOWANCES

In certain circumstances, the local authority may pay an adoption allowance, but this would tend to be the exception rather than the norm. The decision is governed by what costs arise from the additional needs relating to the child's circumstances. The adoption regulations enable any adoption agency to pay an adoption allowance and research has demonstrated the importance of adoption allowances in facilitating adoption for children who would otherwise be unlikely to have the opportunity of a permanent and secure home. Eligibility for an allowance is determined by:

(a) if the adoption is considered to be in the best interests of the child and,

(b) if the adoption would not be practicable without the payment of an allowance.

It should be stressed, however, that an adoption allowance does not include any element of reward or profit, it is purely there to meet a need. Here are some of the specific circumstances in which an allowance might be considered.

(i) If the child has an established relationship with the adopters, for example, via an original placement with them as foster parents. An allowance could be paid if the parents wish to adopt but could not afford to lose the fostering allowance.

(ii) If it is considered in the best interests of the child to be placed with siblings or to join siblings already in a family, or to be placed with an unrelated child with whom he or she has particularly close ties. In other words, in these circumstances the prospective adoptive parents might not have considered having another child, but an allowance would help to make it possible to do so.

(iii) A special needs child may also be eligible for an allowance. If a child has a mental or physical disability, or displays severe emotional or behavioural difficulties, or perhaps a combination of the two, then an allowance could be appropriate to help with costs.

(iv) In the cases where a child needs a special diet, then an allowance would be likely to be made.

(v) It may be possible to receive a subsidy for the replacement of bedding, clothes, shoes etc., if they are used at a higher rate than is usual for a child of a similar age.

(vi) If close supervision for the child's own safety and protection is needed, this again might attract an allowance.

(vii) If specialist assistance is required – regular nursery attendance, possibly with special ancillary assistance, or visits to clinics, or consultants on a routine basis – then it is considered that the expenses should not be the responsibility of the adoptive parents.

Agencies may agree in principle to payment at some future date, if and when the child's condition deteriorates or develops in such a way that it will necessitate higher expenses. Now and again an allowance may be agreed prior to identification of specific adopters. Sometimes in the PPIAS Newsletter you will see that an advertisement for a child is accompanied by the words 'adoption allowance available'.

However, allowances are also linked to the financial circumstances of the adopter, and in some cases it is felt that an allowance is inappropriate, even if it has been previously agreed. The main objective of an agency will be to determine, how much and if any, allowance is appropriate to facilitate a successful placement, and enhance the well-being of the child in the adoptive home. In other words they are looking quite specifically for those sorts of expenses which would not be considered to be normal and familiar items of family expenditure, and at the family's ability to meet such expenses. Certainly adoption should not result in financial hardship or lead to a situation in which the success of the placement is jeopardized because of financial embarrassment. Agencies should give regard to the standard of living of the adopters, and differences should be recognized, but adoption allowances are not intended to subsidize what might be considered a very high standard of living. If an allowance is awarded, it will be reviewed annually arising from a statement from the adopters, or when notified of any change in circumstances in either the child or the adopter. In some circumstances an adoption agency will pay a settling-in grant, to cover such items as beds, bedding, bedroom furnishings and clothing. In other words a one-off payment to establish the child in the family.

4. FOSTERING

There is a complete section at the end of this book with regard to fostering but I think it is worth mentioning here that all agencies pay a fostering allowance, which is related to the age and nature of the difficulties of the child. Increasingly these allowances include a reward element, which is recognition of both the demands made by the child, but also the need of foster carers to be committed to regular attendance at case conferences, reviews etc., and facilitate contacts with the birth family, hospital, therapeutic appointments etc., etc.

These then are the main allowances which are available, or not, as the case may be. There are one or two other points which I think it worth mentioning in connection with the financial aspects of adoption.

1. WILLS

A surprising number of people do not make wills, but it is absolutely essential if you have children to do so, so that there are some safeguards for their future should anything happen to you and your partner. If you do not have a will at the moment, there are a number of good books available on the subject and, of course, you can always go and chat the whole thing through with your solicitor. If you already have children for whom you have made provision, and are now in the process of adopting another child, you need to be aware of the fact that your adopted child will not be covered by your will. This happened to us. When you adopt a child from abroad, you are not allowed to finalize the adoption in the UK for a year after the child has arrived in this country. We suddenly realized that although we had made very careful provision for our other children, because Michael was not actually our child – we were technically only fostering him in the UK – he was not included in our will. We quickly added a codicil to say that he was to be treated in exactly the same way as Charlie, our son by birth, but this is a loophole which it is easy to overlook. We, as a family, believe in appointing guardians although, of course, this is not necessary. We just feel that if we were both killed in a car crash, or whatever, we, with our intimate knowledge of our own children, are the best people to decide what should happen to them. We therefore have it spelt out fairly carefully and the guardians are well aware of what is expected of them. There is no doubt about it, this does provide an element of peace of mind as one battles one's way up the rain soaked M6, with nil visibility, sandwiched between two ten-ton lorries!

2. INSURANCE POLICIES

As with wills, it may well be that you have taken out some form of insurance policy which will be payable to your dependants in the event of your death. Do make sure that your adopted child is included on the policy.

3. PRIVATE MEDICINE

If as a family you subscribe to a private medical scheme then you should have no difficulty in including your adopted child, even before an adoption has been completed. If the child has some specific medical problem, he may well not be covered for that condition, though hopefully all unrelated medical conditions will be. We know a family who adopted a little girl with a hole in the heart. She had a highly successful operation at eleven months and has been given a complete discharge by the Brompton Hospital. She *is* covered under the family's private medical scheme, but all heart and heart related diseases are excluded, which is fair enough.

4. DAY-TO-DAY CARE

It would be wrong to talk about the financial implications of adoption without considering the day-to-day costs of caring for a child. In this I think you need to be very sensitive, both to the child's needs and to your own reaction to parenthood. It may well be that you have tried for many years to have a child and that at last, after years of frustration, you are about to welcome into your home the child whom you are to adopt. The tendency to overwhelm that child with gifts, toys, lovely clothes and a magnificent bedroom – assuming you could afford all these things – must be considerable. It is here that I want to introduce a note of caution. Firstly, the child is going to have to cope with many bewildering experiences in moving into your home. What he will value most is the familiar things – his ragged Teddy, a battered little suitcase, some ancient books and toys. Maybe these, his only possessions look like they need chucking straight in the bin, but for heaven's sake do nothing of the kind. Treasure them as if they were the crown jewels, for they are all your child has in the world.

In the months preceding his coming to live with you permanently, you will have got to know your child fairly well, and certainly you should have a very special present which you know he wants to mark his arrival.

> *I know of a very nice woman, named Susette, now in her late forties who was adopted at nine and still has the doll her adoptive parents gave her on her arrival at their home. She is happily married with three children of her own but that doll is still a very necessary symbol of her emotional happiness. As she says, it stands for the beginning of her real life.*

So by all means have a shiny bike, a doll, a train set, whatever is most appropriate, waiting to mark that very special moment when the child comes home. Of course, gather around you a few other toys, books and games as well, but do not spend a fortune because by far the most valuable way ahead is for you and your child to build his new life *together*. If the child is old enough, this particularly applies to his bedroom. During the visits leading up to the permanent placement, you may well go out and choose curtain material/decide where the bed should go/ what colour carpet he wants/what frieze should go round the walls. It may well be that this is not appropriate until he actually moves in, in which case make the room warm and welcoming but allow him time to put his own personal stamp on it, which may not be at all how you envisaged it.

Children who have been starved of emotional well-being tend to be small in stature. Funnily enough, it is height rather than weight which is the true indicator as to the child's emotional stability. For this reason many children, once settled in an adoptive home, grow like weeds, and so it would be silly to spend a great deal of money on an expensive wardrobe which the child may well grow out of in a few months. Our son admittedly was suffering from malnutrition, but in the first year he was with us he grew eleven inches, which, bearing in mind he was only two, represented well over a third of his overall height. He needed new clothes every month or so! Hand-me-downs are a Godsend. Children's clothes are so expensive and while shoes must be new, most children grow out of their clothes long before they wear them out.

There is also the question of personal taste to consider. Here again it is so much better if the child can choose clothes with you, rather than have you buy them on his behalf. Bearing this in mind, you could acquire a wardrobe of hand-me-downs to keep him going and then gradually replace them with clothes of his choice when his growing and your pocket make it appropriate.

It should also be mentioned that many children – once they are in the security of an adoptive home – need to regress, sometimes almost back to birth. This is a very healthy sign and should be encouraged, and here again for a few months you may well find that the activities and toys being sought are totally inappropriate for the child's age.

This again is where second-hand equipment can be such a help, since buying new would never be properly justified. Similarly you may well adopt a child in an inbetween stage, in other words the child may well be still in a cot but you realize it will only be a few months before she will be ready for a bed. Or that at three, she needs to be transported about in a buggy occasionally on a long shopping expedition, but clearly this will not be necessary in a year's time. Here again, second-hand equipment would seem to be a sensible option.

So, the message is do not smother the child with too many material possessions initially, both for his sake and your own. Take time and do it together as a family.

SECTION 2

Types of adoption

7

Adopting babies and toddlers

Traditionally, when people think of adoption, they think in terms of adopting a baby or possibly a toddler. Certainly the concept of adopting an older child is something which is relatively new and without doubt carries more problems. Babies adopted in the UK almost exclusively go to young couples who have a proven infertility problem and are childless. The exception to this is babies who have a particular health problem or whose prognosis is likely to be troubled in the future. Where possible, it is of course ideal if the baby is adopted straight from hospital. In some instances, where a mother is quite sure she wishes her baby to be adopted at birth, she likes to meet the prospective adoptive parents before the birth. This, of course, can be a very difficult meeting for everyone, particularly for the adoptive parents. Nonetheless, it can be very helpful, particularly when in the years ahead the adopted child wants to know as much as possible about his parents and the circumstances of his adoption. In a way it also involves the future adoptive parents more, so, if you like, they are pregnant too – eagerly awaiting the birth of what will be their child. Certainly in the past this was the traditional way in which adoptions took place. Mothers, usually unmarried, went to a mother and baby home, and the child was then handed straight to its future parents, with no need for foster care in between or any doubts as to the child's future.

In modern times of course, unmarried parenthood carries nothing like the social stigma it did. Contraception is more effective, abortion is more available and this means there are far fewer babies available for adoption immediately after birth. In addition, because there is more help available, many mothers are encouraged to try and keep their babies. This sometimes goes wrong – babies are a great deal easier to look after than toddlers, particularly if the mother is in very tight financial circumstances – perhaps living in bed and breakfast accommodation or in a one-roomed flat. In these circumstances the mother may well cope until the child is walking and then find the burden of motherhood too much for her.

THE PROS AND CONS OF ADOPTING BABIES

The pros

- If you are lucky enough to be able to adopt a very young baby, the child is going to feel so much more like yours than if you adopt an older child.

- You are likely to bond quickly, since physical closeness solves so many of the barriers that can exist between a parent and child trying to form a relationship.

- The baby will fulfil the parents' image of parenthood so

much more readily than an older child.

- It will become far easier to become what could be termed a 'normal' family, than suddenly taking on an older child.

- There is a huge advantage in having the whole of your child's life to enjoy. Speaking for myself and my husband, we deeply regret that we missed the first two years of our son's life (particularly since we know that he went through unimaginable hardships in that period). We will always carry with us a sadness that this is something we missed – and so I think it is with most adoptive parents who grew to love an older child.

The cons

- Because a baby cannot tell you what is wrong, all new parents tend to become somewhat neurotic when they cannot apparently pacify their baby. You know the sort of thing ... we've fed him, we've changed him, we've winded him, he doesn't seem tired ... so why is he still crying? What have we done wrong? I always think along with every child is born a great heap of guilt which parents carry with them for ever. However hard we try to be good parents, in our own eyes we are never quite good enough. It is easy to see how much more vulnerable you are in the role of adoptive parent. The child is screaming and you cannot stop him, and you do not know what is wrong. Instantly you will assume it is because you are not the child's natural mother or father, and that if you were, you would know what to do. Of course this is not the case, but it is how many couples feel in moments of tension. An older child can at least explain his problem.

- You will find that there is a tendency to undervalue yourself as a parent simply because you did not actually produce the child. This feeling can be intensified by tactless grandparents, aunts, even friends. Everyone is eager to give advice to you as a new mum and dad, the feeling being that you need it more because you did not give birth to the child yourselves. You must fight this instinctive sense of inferiority for all you are worth. Just think how many natural parents abuse and neglect their children. Parents are not born, they are made, and indeed I would go so far as to say that in many instances adoptive parents are better than natural parents, because they have had to give so much more thought to the decision to become parents.

- There is also a tendency for adoptive parents of babies to be over-anxious about their baby's health. Initially, they will still have the sense of this baby being someone else's child and every time the baby has a slight sniffle or appears to be unwell, there will be a tendency for them to be thrown into a state of panic. They may also feel that their doctor and health visitor are scrutinizing them more carefully than they would ordinary parents, and the combination of all this can lead to an enormous amount of tension which, of course, in turn makes the baby less settled and creates a vicious circle.

My advice to any couple embarking on the adoption of a baby is to try and approach it as 'normally' as possible. Buy magazines about parenthood, buy all the parentcraft books, talk to your friends who have babies. You might well find it more relaxing to learn to bath the baby of a friend than to go to parentcraft classes, where you feel everyone is curious because you are not pregnant. Men and women have raised babies through the centuries in the most dire circumstances and against all odds. In today's world, it really is not such a daunting task. Of course it is tiring, worrying, emotional and very, very demanding but it is such a joy. If you find yourself in the position of adopting a baby, concentrate on that joy. Babyhood is over so quickly, do not waste time wondering whether you are good enough – just have fun. Here are some case histories which give an indication of the sort of circumstances in which babies become available for adoption. The first of these stories is about a very straightforward adoption.

Mark was born in hospital, in December last. His mother, Annie was seventeen and homeless. Annie left her own home after her mother re-married. She had difficulties getting along with her step-father and his two younger children, and one day simply left. For a year she lived on the streets, became involved both in drugs and alcohol abuse. Mark's father was twenty-eight and also homeless, following discharge from the Army. His name was Dennis. Annie and Dennis met in a night shelter and in fact it was a night-shelter worker who some months later realized that Annie was pregnant and took her to an ante-natal clinic. Right from the beginning, Mark's future was destined to be relatively straightforward because Annie wanted to cooperate and wanted the best for her baby. She knew she could not cope with him and as well as being prepared to attend ante-natal clinic to ensure the baby remained in good health, she also was prepared to take her HIV test, which proved negative, and made adoption much easier.

> When Mark was born he was placed immediately with Peter (twenty-seven) and Jackie (twenty-five). Peter is an assistant manager at the Co-op and Jackie works in a building society as a cashier. They are a childless couple, and in their case were perhaps lucky in as much that they were able to identify their infertility early because Jackie has simply never ovulated. The placement has worked wonderfully well. Peter and Jackie have a very stable marriage and Mark has had a happy, stable childhood right from the very beginning.
>
> The one difficult moment for everyone was when Annie asked if she could see Jackie and Peter prior to the birth. The meeting went well but it was obviously a strain for everyone concerned. Via the adoption agency, it was agreed that there would be an exchange of photographs in the future, which Annie found very reassuring.
>
> This adoption, of course, was greatly facilitated by Annie's very mature approach to her pregnancy, despite her extreme youth. One can only hope that in the years ahead, Annie's life achieves the same sort of stability, and love, which she has made possible for her son.

Sasha's adoption was not quite as straightforward. The main reason being that the prognosis of her development is uncertain.

> Sasha's mother, Theresa, is thirty-two but has severe learning disabilities and a mental age of eight. Theresa lives with her elderly parents in a small village. Sasha's father, David, is forty-two, married and of average intelligence. The story of Sasha's conception is a shocking one. Theresa attended an Adult Training Centre, travelling by coach each day. David was the coach driver, and as Theresa was the last person to be dropped

off at the end of the run, there was some time during which David and Theresa were on their own, with the result that regular intercourse took place between them, on the coach. Although, of course, what David was doing was not strictly illegal, there were very strong similarities to abusing a child, which he recognized in as much that he gave Theresa sweets as a reward and told her what was happening was 'their secret'. Eventually Theresa became pregnant. Being a fairly large woman and not, of course, aware herself of what had happened to her, by the time the pregnancy was discovered, there was no question of an abortion.

Her parents were not able to cope – caring for Theresa alone was already stretching their resources in every way, and clearly Theresa was not capable of looking after a child herself. After the birth, Sasha was placed with temporary foster parents while her future was decided. David made no attempt to become involved. Although there were no obvious signs of mental retardation it was recognized that there was a strong possibility that Sasha might be affected by her mothers's problems, although there was no history of mental illness on either side of the family.

At four and a half months old Sasha was placed with Jo and Sarah, who were thirty-three and thirty-six respectively. Jo is a storeman and Sarah a nurse, and therefore by virtue of her training, well able to cope with Sasha should learning difficulties arise. Jo and Sarah have been married for ten years. It is a second marriage for Sarah, there were no children from the previous marriage, and Jo has a low sperm count hence they were likely to remain childless.

At the time of writing this book it would appear that Sasha, now two and a half, has average intelligence.

THE PROS AND CONS OF ADOPTING TODDLERS

The Pros

Much of what has been said about babies applies to toddlers, in as much that early on in the relationship it is possible to develop a very real sense of belonging between parent and adoptive child, which is more difficult with older children. Against this, of course, toddlers have had that much longer to be damaged by their previous environment. It may simply be that they have been with one set of foster parents since birth and the sheer disruption to their young lives of moving away from the only home they have ever known into yours, can cause a great deal of heartache. More likely, however, they will have suffered some degree of deprivation in the hands of their natural parents, and may well then have spent a period with foster parents before coming to you, the adoptive parents.

A social worker once said to me that she reckoned that for every year of neglect and deprivation, a child needed a year of secure home life to put things right. If this is so, then the baby you adopt at fourteen months is likely to be well on course to normal childhood by the time he is three. Certainly this would be our experience.

When we adopted Michael from Romania he was twenty-five months old, but he could neither walk, talk nor stand and he came out of the orphanage wearing clothes for a three-month-old baby. We assumed that we would have years of difficulties ahead while he caught up with his peers, if indeed he ever did. In fact, it took him less than a year to reach most of his targets and in some respects, as little as just a few months. By the time he was four, his past was well and truly behind him – physically, mentally and emotionally.

As our experience indicates, a big advantage in adopting a toddler is that however distressing his life has been to date, the chances are you will be able to put things right for him.

The cons

Perhaps one of the greatest difficulties surrounding the adoption of toddlers is that you take on your child at a time he is more volatile than he will be at any other time during his childhood, with the exception of adolescence. Having had toddlers and adolescents in the house at the same time, I can assure you that there are a great many similarities! Both periods in childhood represent huge stepping stones. Toddlers are moving from babyhood into childhood, adolescents from childhood into adulthood – one moment they wish they were in babyhood/childhood, the next they are furious with you because you are not allowing them to develop into children/adults. It is a 'no win' situation and often extremely difficult to handle well, however experienced you are.

For new first-time parents confronted with the screaming rages that only a two-year-old in full cry can produce, it can be very worrying. This cannot be normal, they inevitably will feel. Where are we going wrong? It is hard to believe that this is the sort of behaviour that they could reasonably expect from any toddler, however secure his past. If you are in the running for adopting a child between the years of one and three, then I suggest you read every book you can on toddlers and make it your business to visit friends with pre-school children, particularly between the dreaded hours of 4pm and 6pm, when they are likely to be at their very worst. After a few sessions of this, by the time you take delivery of your own child, you will probably consider his or her behaviour to be saint-like by comparison!

Seriously though, caring for a toddler is a very strenuous, exhausting, frustrating business at times, whether the child is adopted or not. Try to relax, try not to enter into the battles of wills and have the gin bottle standing by for when the child is safely tucked up in bed and asleep. You are going to need the odd swig! Then, miraculously, somewhere between two-and-a-half and three-and-a-half, like the butterfly emerging from the chrysalis, suddenly out will pop the child – still infuriating, still self-opinionated but a little person who can be talked to and reasoned with. Even more astonishing, you will realize that all those months of battles have actually cemented the relationship and helped build the love – for love thrives just as well on shared times of difficulty as on shared times of happiness.

It has to be said that it is not uncommon for the 'system' to cause a child to be adopted as a toddler rather than as a baby. All too often, unnecessary delays do seem to take place, which cause children a great deal of distress. Alex's story is a case in point.

Alex's mother, Michelle, was thrown out of the family home in early adolescence – her mother maintaining that she was beyond parental control. Certainly Michelle had problems – she played truant from school, was caught shoplifting and was very promiscuous. Whether, though, her mother was unable or unwilling to care for her it is hard to tell. A series of resident placements were found for Michelle but she became increasingly violent. At one point a social worker and her husband attempted to offer her foster care but even this broke down.

When Michelle was sixteen she became pregnant by a black US Air Force man. The child, Shelley, remained with Michelle for three months, under the close supervision of a social worker with a degree of help from the social worker who had fostered her. Michelle and Shelley lived in a house with two other girls which, of course, was not ideal and at three months there was found to be bruising on Shelley and an unconvincing explanation as to how it had happened. Shelley was taken into care and placed with foster parents, where she remained for fourteen months.

During this period Michelle visited her daughter regularly and eventually the two were reunited in a family unit, which is a home where mothers and their children can be given a degree of supervised care. By this time, however, Michelle was pregnant again by a white man she had met at a party. Michelle decided that she would put all her energies into Shelley and would have the new baby adopted. In any event it is probable that the baby would have been removed at birth, since it was not considered possible for Michelle to care for two children. The father of the unborn baby was very co-operative with the Social Services in providing background information and had no objection to the child being adopted. Alex was born when Michelle was twenty and his half-sister, Shelley, four. He was immediately fostered and seen by his mother every two months. When he was ten months old, there was a full hearing as to Alex's future and Michelle refused to give consent for him to be adopted. Apparently this is a classic case of reluctance to sign away a child, although realistically there is no possibility of caring for him. A further hearing date was set and eventually, at fourteen months old, Alex was placed with Pat and Stephen.

Pat, at thirty-six, was a teacher and Stephen, an AA man, was thirty-seven. Pat had had an ectopic pregnancy which had irrevocably damaged her fallopian tube and it was thought unlikely that she would ever have children. Alex was their first child and there were major difficulties at the time of him being introduced to them, because of his enormous attachment to his foster family. As far as he was concerned, they were his mum and dad, and at fourteen months found a change of family absolutely intolerable. Pat and Stephen were naturally very undermined in confidence by Alex's rejection of them and it was only by an enormous amount of perseverence on all sides that eventually Alex settled down and he is now a happy, well adjusted child.

The question one has to ask is why it took the Social Services fourteen months to place Alex when, clearly, before he was even born it was established that there was no way Michelle could ever care for him? All along his father had given full support to Alex being adopted. There can be so many long-term damaging effects in this sort of handling of a child. Will Pat and Stephen always feel they are second best as far as Alex is concerned?

As we will see when we discuss the adoption of school age children, decisions concerning permanent placement in this country do seem to take such a time to organize, often causing terrible suffering to the children. Of course, not all toddlers will have the same sort of problems as Alex, though one could say that in fact he was lucky – at least he had known nothing but love and security in his first fourteen months of life, whereas many toddlers will have been in and out of care and suffered all sorts of abuse and neglect. What I think is important is not to underestimate the depth of understanding which really very young children have. I can quote from my own experiences here.

> As I mentioned, when we adopted Michael from Romania, he was two, although physically he appeared more like a tiny baby. In the period between our finding him and being able to bring him home to England he had to stay permanently in the orphanage. Although the care he was receiving was negligible, we were not allowed to remove him until our Romanian adoption was complete. We therefore employed an elderly couple living nearby to go in and visit Michael twice a day, to give him a good meal, change his clothes and bathe his sores. They were also able to give him plenty of cuddles and some much needed fresh air, outside the stench of the orphanage. By bribing the orphanage staff, the elderly couple were even able to take him back to their own flat on Sundays, which was as well because on Sundays, in Romania, the orphanage children receive virtually no care at all, as there is only a skeleton staff on duty.
>
> Eight weeks after finding him, the great day came and Michael was released from the orphanage. The whole family came out to collect him. We had to spend several days in Bucharest, waiting for a flight home. They were valuable days – we were, if you like, on neutral territory and it gave everybody a change to get to know one another. On our last day, we went and had a farewell party with the old couple at their flat, who by now were known as Granny and Grandpa. When it came to leave, we had a very emotional parting – on our part we know that they had been responsible for keeping our son alive, and they in turn had become very fond of their little Michael. Michael allowed himself to be kissed and seemed quite cheerful until we got into the car. Then,

leaning against my shoulder, he stared out of the back window and waved and waved at Granny and Grandpa, long after they had gone from our sight. He didn't cry but his face was very solemn and full of a great sadness. He was only two but he knew something monumental was about to happen to him and that his old life had come to an end. You may think that I am being fanciful but we all sensed it. He couldn't speak our language, indeed he couldn't speak at all, but he knew from that moment his life was changing for ever.

We do have this tendency to talk over the heads of tiny children playing on the floor, assuming that because their speech may not be very good, their understanding may be correspondingly deficient. This, though, is often not the case and months later you will have a conversation repeated to you verbatim, which at the time you'd never thought they understood.

On the one hand your toddler may well need to be treated like a baby, to recapture the loving he has never had. On the other, he may have an understanding apparently beyond his years, and you may find these violent swings very confusing. And if you are confused, just imagine how he feels!

Caring for your toddler will be rather like walking a tightrope with a bucket of custard on your head – but the rewards are beyond rubies.

8

Adopting school-age children

By far the greatest number of children available for adoption are those of school age. All through babyhood up until the age of four to five, the number of people seeking to adopt outweighs the number of children available. But from school age onwards, quite the reverse applies – there are too many children and too few parents. Having said that, in many respects the current system does not seem to reflect the urgent needs of these children. As we have discussed in earlier chapters, the vetting process for prospective parents is not only onerous but lengthy, and matching school age children with prospective adoptive parents seems to be a very unwieldy and again, lengthy, process. Of course it is not easy. Children who have reached the school years usually have accumulated a sackful of problems – experienced too many moves and changes and acquired many behavioural difficulties. Nonetheless, it seems that so much of childhood can be lost in a state of limbo, while the bureaucratic wheels roll on.

As I have previously mentioned, one of the problems

associated with the adoption of older children is that until you have been linked with a child, you cannot even meet that child. Most prospective parents find it relatively easy to bond with a young baby or toddler so this method is not such a problem there. However, a child of school age is completely different. From the very start it is much more of a two-way relationship. The child will have built up in her mind her own image of how her parents should be, just as you will have your image of your child. When expectations differ very much from the reality, inevitably there are going to be problems. However, under the current system there is no machinery, if you like, for allowing the natural chemistry between people to be a major factor in the permanent placing of children. No one for one moment would suggest that in seeking one's marriage partner, you should first be linked on paper to a specific person and only meet as the final link in the chain – except, of course, in countries where arranged marriages still apply. Yet this is effectively what is expected of both parents and children, and I believe the system is flawed. People need to meet, talk, exchange ideas whether they are six, sixteen or sixty – parents and children need to know whether they want to spend time together, whether they are interested in each other. There was a time when adoption parties used to be arranged by some agencies, where children cleared for adoption and approved adoptive parents could meet in the informal atmosphere of a children's party. I think it is rather a good idea, though some people would say it is like a cattle market. I suppose the truth is there is no easy answer to the problem. All you, as prospective parents, can do is to try in the linking process to find a child with whom you know you have a number of common points of interest.

Until recently, we were trying to adopt a school age child from the UK, to join our family. We were being seriously considered for one little girl whose background is very, very different from our other childrens'. However, she is very sporty and adores games, as do our other children. She is also particularly keen on animals and our home is over-run with them.

This then is the kind of common ground for which you are seeking. You can do no more until you meet.

As already mentioned, school age children inevitably come with what the Social Services term a degree of 'baggage'. In other words, unlike younger children they are bound to carry problems with them and these problems tend to fall into quite specific categories. Let us look at some of the problems you are likely to encounter. I must stress, however, that not all children suffer from these and certainly no child has all of them! It is just a guide as to what may happen:

THE HONEYMOON PERIOD

Many older children arriving at their adoptive family for the first time will be desperately anxious to please initially. Particularly during the visits prior to coming to live permanently in the family, everyone will be on their best behaviour, and it is difficult for the situation not to appear false at times. For some children this honeymoon period may go on for weeks or months. For some children it is just a question of days or even hours. Certainly you will not need to be told when it is over!

The comfort you can take when suddenly your sweet, biddable child appears to have gone, is that now you are really starting to slog up the coal face of parenthood. The honeymoon period may have come as a delightful surprise after what you had been led to expect, but it is not real life. The next stage, the testing time, should be welcomed as progress, although at the time it certainly will not feel like it!

THE TESTING TIME

The testing time may take all sorts of different forms according to the type of child and the experiences that she has been through. The basic theme behind it, though, is likely to be the child's own sense of self-worth. Children take on board a great deal of responsibility for what happens to them. If their birth parents mistreat them, they tend to think it is their fault. If they are taken away from their family, they often think of it as a punishment, not seeing it as something done in their own interests and for their own safety. When they are moved from one foster carer to the next, although the reasons may be totally unconnected with them but because of a problem within the foster family, they will take the blame. So often inadequate explanations as to what is happening next are passed on to the children, with the result that they become more and more confused, and equally certain that the whole thing is their fault and that they are bad.

The testing time, therefore – whatever form it takes – will be the child's attempt to see to what degree she can push you before you reject her. She will be convinced that you will reject her, that it is only a matter of time, and she may push you to the very brink of tolerance. Early on, of course, it is terribly important to stress and stress again that whatever she does, you are always going to be there for her, always love her and that you are now a forever family. But she will not believe you. Most children have been let down again and again, they have no reason to have any faith and so they will persevere in their reign of terror, to try and break you, to try and prove you are just like all the rest. It goes without saying that this can be a nightmare period – the child may have tantrums of unbelievable proportions and smash everything in sight, particularly if she thinks any of the items have special meaning for you. The child may run away or physically abuse you. There will be so much anger at what has happened to her, yet at the same time so much fear at being hurt again. However much you understand the reasons for the behaviour, it may not make it any easier to tolerate. The only advice that can be given is that somehow you must hang in there, and to remember that you are not alone. Social workers have seen all this before and are there to help.

REGRESSION

For many children who have had an inadequate childhood and babyhood, there may be the very strong feeling that they need to almost crawl back into the womb and start again with you, their forever family. This is a very good sign, although it can be extremely confusing for parents. Suddenly you may have a seven-year-old crawling about on the floor, or demanding a bottle, wanting to be cradled like a baby, wrapped up in a rug. Some people may find this difficult to handle, embarrassing even, but it is important. So many of these children have learnt to cope alone, have learnt not to need a close relationship with anyone, and in these circumstances unless they can be allowed to regress, this independent streak will damage their ability to make emotional attachments in the future. They will be far more likely to have failed marriages and unsatisfactory relationships with their own children.

So if your child seeks to behave much younger than his age, do encourage it. It will not last long – a few weeks or a few months at the most, but it is a very valuable exercise in the bonding process. Whatever you do, do not consider it as a period of deterioration. It is actually a great step forward in your child's emotional development.

DIVIDE AND RULE

Some children will take readily to one parent and not to the other, and this can be a very hurting and damaging experience. Surprisingly, a little girl who has perhaps been sexually abused by her father will not be necessarily frightened of men, in fact quite the contrary. She may be particularly attentive to her new adoptive father and hostile towards her mother. There are various theories about this. Possibly, in these circumstances, the child will feel that her mother betrayed her, that when her father was doing these horrible things to her, her mother should have stopped it. Therefore her aggressive feelings will not be directed towards father figures but mother figures, who failed to help her when she needed it. This is a very difficult problem and it is desperately important that parents provide a united front and that the parent who is apparently being rejected is given as much support as possible by the parent who is accepted. Only time will heal this one; time and consistency of attitude towards the child. The only comfort I can offer is that it is a very normal problem and one which usually adjusts itself fairly quickly.

INDISCRIMINATE AFFECTION

Some children – usually those who are apparently talkative and sociable – make inappropriate physical overtures to almost complete strangers – climbing on their laps, hugging and kissing them, even telling them they love them. Clearly a child who reacts like this has an attachment problem and it is difficult for prospective adoptive parents to feel close to their child if their child greets everyone in the same way. Of course what the child is really saying is not that I love everyone, but that I need to be loved. As the weeks go by and she begins to realize that at last there is someone important in her life, that there are two people who really care about her, then she will start to discriminate.

This happened to us with Michael. When he first came home from Romania he appeared to love life and everyone in it. He threw his arms around everyone, from his brother and sister to the postman. Yet three months later he was like a limpet – he clung to me wherever I went. I couldn't go out of his sight, leave the room, even to go to the lavatory without him screaming for me. This too, of course, was an over-reaction, but in time he adjusted, so that he knew who the important people were in his life, but could trust them when out of his sight.

DESPERATE DESIRE TO PLEASE

Some children seem to stay in a perpetual honeymoon period. They are desperately anxious to please and agree with everything anyone says. If asked to express an opinion, usually they say they do not know, because they are worried about saying the wrong thing. They will probably be very neat, extremely quiet and will be terrified of doing anything wrong. An upset glass of juice will be a complete catastrophe in their lives. This sort of behaviour is actually very upsetting for parents, because whilst a child keeps up this barrier of goodness, it is almost impossible to get to know him properly. This silent, attentive, obedient little stranger is no one with whom you can have a proper relationship. It does help enormously in these circumstances if there are other children in the family, because gradually the child will see that normal childhood pranks are quite acceptable and so may start to copy them. If the child is an only child it is far more difficult and only by very gentle encouragement will the child gradually relax and start to behave normally. Just recently one adoptive mother was telling me of the day her adopted little girl picked up a bowl of jelly and threw it at her brother.

> *The plate smashed, there was jelly everywhere but Ted, her husband, and I just sat there and cried our eyes out. We had been waiting for Barbara to do something bad for nine long months. Of course we all ended up in fits of laughter, it was so ludicrous – knee-deep in jelly, crying our eyes out – what a sight we must have looked. But it was the beginning. She is a right little imp now but I wouldn't have her any other way. That silent, obedient stranger nearly killed us.*

OVER-COMPETENCY

Some children are really parents to themselves – they have needed to be. Children as young as five get up, make their own beds and tidy their rooms without being asked. It sounds wonderful? Maybe, but it is not normal. These children loathe having to ask for help and in fact they never do. The most they are likely to do is grant their parents permission to do something for them. Some have younger siblings who they boss about. Here again, getting a child to relax, to hand over management of him or herself to you can be a very slow process, but the relief ultimately is enormous. Terry, talking about her seven year old adopted daughter, Sam, says:

> *It is extraordinary really, we have some photographs taken of Sam in her first week with us. It was right at the beginning of summer – here was this very serious, grown-up little child staring into the lens of the camera. By autumn she was almost unrecognizable – she had grown a great deal, as I know to my cost; new clothes, new shoes – but extraordinarily, she looked much younger than the springtime child, years younger in fact. It was not just us who thought this, many people commented on it. It was as if all the responsibilities she'd had heaped on her shoulders prematurely, had just slipped away. It's lovely really, what it means is we have given her back her childhood. Before she was a miniature adult, taking full responsibility for herself.*

LACK OF SELF-AWARENESS

Some children, particularly those who have been abused, are frighteningly unaware of their own bodies and their bodily functions. This may be expressed by over-eating to the point where they are almost sick, or by failing to go to the lavatory because they are not aware that they need to do so, even though they may have crippling stomach ache.

Some also seem unaware of extremes of temperature. It seems to me that they have trained themselves to pay no attention to the signals from their own body and this in turn alleviates the discomforts that they would otherwise feel. This certainly applied in Romania. Many of the children in the orphanages had been subjected over a long period of time to both malnutrition, with all its associate discomforts, and also extremes of temperature. The result was that some of the children seemed to have an incredibly high pain threshold. One mother told me of how her little son had his fingers accidentally crushed in a door jamb by his sister, but was completely unaware that it was happening – he was somehow able to blank it off. To a lesser extent, this may be something you notice in your child, but it will right itself in time.

HYPERACTIVITY AND AGGRESSION

Some children with a very insecure past become hyperactive – constantly on the move and often very aggressive with it; kicking, biting, scratching. There are two problems – firstly the parents have to learn how to physically manage the child without hurting him and becoming hurt themselves, and secondly they have to remedy the condition. Trial and error will be involved here. Certainly all hyperactive children need a structured environment and some children do seem to respond to an additive-free diet, details of which you will probably be able to find out from your doctor. Parents of a hyperactive child understandably, often feel that they need space and time away from the child, but at the same time they must be careful not to look as if they are rejecting the child by sending him away – punishing him, for example, by shutting him in his room will seem like rejection. The reverse is the best way to handle him – he needs constant communication, prolonged cuddles, physical contact, and you in turn will need to put away every single item you possess which is in any way precious until this stage is over!

FAECAL SOILING

One of the most distressing complaints for parents is children who soil themselves, in many cases apparently on purpose. Sometimes they smear the walls or their beds, sometimes they appear not to care at all, other times they hide their soiled underwear. This is a difficult problem to solve, one which is likely to make you very angry, and you will probably need the help of your social worker. Suffice to say that this complaint is connected with unexpressed anger and if the child can just learn to off-load anger in some other way, then gradually the problem will disappear.

SELF-MUTILATION

Sometimes children will mutilate themselves by trying, say, to cut their wrists. This may be done largely for effect but again it causes enormous distress to the parents as well as the child. It may be an indicator of some psychotic illness and here again you should immediately make your social worker aware of what is going on, as you are likely to need professional help.

SLEEP PROBLEMS

All children have nightmares from time to time, but some children, who have suffered particularly traumatic periods in their life, will suffer from very severe night terrors, where they wake up screaming in panic. Problems at night may also include night roaming. When children feel lonely and depressed, they may often wander around the house at night to the point where it may be necessary for parents to either fix a lock on the door, or at any rate use an intercom system for the child's own protection.

All problems at night-time, if they are regular, tend to suggest that the child is anxious or worried about something. Whilst it is important not to develop too much habit-forming contact at night, parents do need to recognize that these terrors are very real and, however briefly, must comfort and reassure the child.

These then are some of the problems you might have to face with a school age child. I hope this chapter has not proved too daunting. Try to relax and in the early days, do try not to judge the child's behaviour too critically or set it against your own standards. Try above all to put yourself in the child's position. Imagine what it must be like to perhaps have reached the age of eight, having experienced six or seven different moves in your life, as between natural parents, children's homes and foster parents. Often in the middle of what you must have thought was a normal day, someone will have arrived and simply taken you away from the life you have become used to and plonked you down somewhere else, with little or no explanation. What must that feel like, to have to start all over again? We all know how we feel ourselves, faced with a new school, a new job, a holiday in a place we have never visited before. It's quite an effort, isn't it, learning where everything is, learning how everybody else behaves, learning who is who? For most of us, though, home remains the same – we might well move house, the family may have its ups and downs, but most things remain constant. Children are so helpless, they have no control over their own lives, and people make decisions for them, often without even consulting them. They are shunted around from pillar to post like so much baggage and then everyone sits back and wonders why they are disturbed. In difficult days, after you have taken delivery of your school age child, try and put yourself in his shoes and recognize how brave he was when he arrived on your doorstep for the first time, how well he coped with having his life turned upside down. Most children are amazing when it comes to their powers of adaptability. Rather like sick children, children who have been the subject of a deprived childhood do have the most astonishing ability to put their problems behind them and start afresh. To help them to do so, has to be one of the most rewarding jobs on earth.

9

Adopting older children and teenagers

Taking responsibility for an adolescent, or a child approaching adolescence, is no small undertaking. Adolescence is a confusing time, even if you come from the most stable of family backgrounds. Most of us can still remember it! You feel so inadequate, so insecure and so angry at your own vulnerability. One minute you want to shake off the shackles of parents and home and strike off on your own, the next you long to be cuddled up in bed with a favourite teddy. Ask most people what period of their life they would like to go back to – some favour childhood, some their early twenties, but *nobody* wants to be a teenager again.

For children who come from a confused and deprived family background, adolescence often comes early. These children have had plenty of exposure to most aspects of adult life, and may well have been almost entirely responsible for themselves for some years. Often they are very sexually aware for their age and have a veneer of independence and sophistication, which must not be mistaken for confidence, because most of these children are very frightened inside.

Older children and adolescents for whom permanent placements are being sought, almost invariably are children who came into care when much younger and who, for whatever reason, have had a history of previous placements that either went wrong or at any rate were terminated – probably causing considerable distress to the child. In other words, the older child tends to be a very disturbed child. Of course, this is not always the case. It could be that a child who has been living with foster parents for some years decides that she would like to formalize the relationship by being adopted. This could be a lovely arrangement for all concerned – a celebration if you like of the child's and foster parents' commitment to one another – a very happy outcome.

There are very few children over fourteen for whom adoptive families are actively being sought. The way it normally works is that long-term fostering is considered most appropriate for a teenager and it is only if the child specifically requests to be adopted that adoption would be considered.

As I mentioned briefly in a previous chapter, I think there is far too much exclusive emphasis placed on the relationship between child and parent during childhood, and insufficient importance attributed to the role of a parent once the child has grown up. If a child has had a very disturbed life and eventually is found a permanent placement – let's say at fourteen or fifteen – I think it is wonderful if that placement can lead to adoption ... even though adoption may take place only a year or two before the child comes of age. Parenting should be forever. Grown-up children need a base to come back to, to bring their friends, ultimately their husband or wife, and, of course, their children. Everyone should have grandparents. The world is a very confusing place. To have a yardstick against which to judge situations and people is a wonderful asset to have as one matures. Above all to have a place where you belong, where you are accepted no matter what, to be able to go home when your girlfriend's 'given you the elbow', when you've lost your job, when you feel ill or to celebrate your new job, your engagement ... Most of us at almost any age, would love a bit of mothering on occasions, and it is all the more important if you have missed out in the early years.

I cannot help feeling that more attention should be given to older children and teenagers with a view to trying to provide them with permanent families. Certainly, if you think this is an area where you could help, the need is huge.

Here is a story of a child for whom adoption came relatively late, but very happily.

Simon is the youngest of three children, born to a white mother and a West Indian father. His parents had never been married and his father, Charlie, had a large number of partners, with the result that Simon had many half-siblings. His mother, Janey, had alcohol problems but she was strongly attached to the children, although the home was chaotic. The children were frequently left alone, or were involved with groups of adults under the influence of alcohol and drugs. They witnessed much overt sexual activity and violence. Sometimes the children and their mother were under siege because Charlie could become very violent and there was a real danger of serious injury.

Simon's elder sister, May, assumed the mothering role for him as their mother deteriorated. Eventually all three children were removed from the home when Simon was nine, and spent the best part of a year in a residential children's home. This was not ideal but at least the children were together. During this period, several attempts were made to rehabilitate them with their mother, but each failed and gradually Janey disappeared for longer and longer periods.

Eventually all three children were removed to foster carers, some eighty miles away from their home. The foster carers were a childless white couple, with two other foster children – both girls. They certainly had their hands full with three siblings of mixed parentage – intelligent, challenging and with a surprisingly positive sense of self-worth, derived from their mother in the early days, when things had not been too bad. The children stayed with the foster parents for two years, during which time there was some contact with Janey, and the foster parents went to great lengths to encourage her to visit the children.

Simon, of course, was the only boy in the family, with two sisters and two foster sisters. A very masculine child, he was frequently in confrontation with his foster father, but having said that, there was a strong bond between them which developed as a result of shared interests and a strong male alliance. Simon, probably modelling on Charlie, had a macho approach to life and was very patronizing towards females. He tended to be ostentatious, and although only eleven had a very powerful and forceful personality.

Just before his twelfth birthday, Simon was discovered simulating sexual intercourse with his youngest sister and it emerged that this had been a regular occurrence, not only with her but also with his two foster sisters who were of low intelligence. His foster parents were appalled and felt they simply could not cope with this. As a result, Simon was separated from his sisters for the first time and put back into a children's home, where he remained for two years.

Simon's case was extensively advertised but the only response came from another white couple, whose home was in a multi-racial area, and close to Simon's original home where, of course, many of his extended family still lived.

Simon's new foster parents, Will and Tina, had one eighteen-year-old daughter. Tina is a teacher in a special unit for children with moderate learning difficulties, and had been teaching in a comprehensive school with a significant number of children from different ethnic origins. It was felt therefore that she would understand Simon's particular needs. Will is a publisher. Simon moved in, but initially, not without problems. He retained a continuing attachment to his previous foster carers, despite the fact that they had rejected him and did not want to see him again. Unfavourable comparisons between both families were always being made and, of course, maintaining contact with his sisters was not easy. His lack of respect for women continued and this reflected badly on Tina and her daughter, Sally. He was also very demanding on time. He still had a very strong, ostentatious streak which resulted in him making completely unrealistic demands for material goods. Initially, he also seemed unable to make any kind of emotional response. Nonetheless, Tina and Will were determined to make it work. They went to enormous lengths to help Simon, even having his mother to stay on occasions overnight, to help maintain the bond between mother and son. Gradually, Simon began to calm down. It emerged that he was living with the expectation of being *rejected again and once this did not happen, he began to visibly relax. Once he had been with Tina and Will for more than the two-year period he had been with his previous foster parents, he seemed to feel he had 'made it', that he really wasn't going to be sent away again. It was not until he was nearly fifteen that he broached the idea of adoption. Tina and Will were surprised but extremely touched, and having befriended Janey, Simon found that she, too, was completely in favour of such a move. Simon is now officially adopted and at sixteen, is a much more secure, confident and loving boy, with much of his early aggression gone now that he feels safe.*

As you can see from Simon's story, it was his very vulnerability that was making him so aggressive and this is the case with many teenagers. If you are thinking of trying to foster or adopt a teenage child, you should not be looking primarily at a parenting role, but concentrating instead on friendship. Older children do need to be approached very carefully. At a time when they are normally looking outside their families, imposing on them strict house rules and heavy discipline, will only have them rebelling. As with any relationship, the starting point should be getting to know and understand them, and only then throwing up the odd piece of fencing where you feel it is appropriate.

Self-image is everything for the teenager – they must look good to their peers. This means that not only do they need the right clothes and the right music, they also need to have what the other kids have ... and that usually includes parents, and a home. The breakthrough point with older children is when they start to bring their friends home. This is really important. If you are considering offering your home to a teenager, then you must recognize that it must be to your teenager's friends as well. The day your child walks in with a bunch of friends and feels confident enough to help himself to the contents of the fridge, rather than being irritated, you should be feeling very pleased with yourself because it means he's come home.

As with younger children, some older children and teenagers will need to regress and here you can only take your cue from them. Certainly your job is to take as many pressures off them as you can, solve as many problems for them as you can, and then gradually hand back to them responsibility for their own lives, as and when they want to and feel they can cope.

One of the problems associated with taking on older children is that, by definition, you will probably already have children, either of your own or adopted, or fostered. Some couples with absolutely no experience of parenting might feel that they are experienced enough to take on an older child. However, by far the majority of parents taking on older children, are couples who already have parenting experience. The problems here, of course, is that the child you will be introducing to your home could prove a very disruptive influence. This is fair enough if there is only you and your partner to consider, but what about your other children? You could find that your whole family is under threat. This was the case with Eddie, whose story is very sad.

> *Eddie was the only child of a single woman from a middle-class, academic background. His mother, Fiona, was less intelligent and able than her brother and sister, and from an early age was considered to be a disappointment to her parents. Although she had the benefit of a private education, she left school with no formal qualifications. A fairly unattractive young woman, she had*

very poor self-esteem, which was not helped by the continued criticism of her parents, who seemed to lack any feeling of warmth towards her.

Fiona established herself in her own flat and worked part-time with disabled children. This, of course, did not earn her much money and so she remained financially dependent on her parents, which again did not help her self-image. She had a series of very unsatisfactory relationships with men, apparently having an almost insatiable desire for sex, brought on, probably, by a need to be loved.

She decided that she wanted a child. Having no permanent partner, she entered into a contract with a boyfriend who had a history of depression – an unemployed, artistic, fairly ineffectual young man. He undertook to exert no rights of paternity and he signed a letter to this effect.

Eddie was born fit and healthy and was cared for very well by Fiona, as a baby and very small child. Their relationship, though, was rather claustrophobic, and as the years passed Fiona increasingly suffered from depression, with the result that she ceased to be able to maintain much domestic order. She was very indulgent of Eddie – there was no routine or discipline. As he started to grow up, he developed into a companion for his mother and quickly became old beyond his years, assuming an almost caring role. He had little capacity to play or relate to other children and having inherited his mother's looks, was not an attractive child.

When Eddie was eight, his mother was killed in a car accident in which he was a passenger. An aunt who was living in Italy, came to the UK immediately to care for Eddie, but after a few months said that her own commitments prevented her from being able to take care of him on a permanent basis, and so she returned to Italy. Eddie's grandparents were too elderly to care for him. It was therefore decided that Eddie would have to be taken into care, although his grandparents did request ongoing contact with him.

Eddie was placed with experienced foster carers, from a very contrasting social background to his own. The foster family had grown up children of their own and three adolescent foster children. A warm, loving but very down-to-earth family, there was no emphasis on reading or music or other features of Eddie's previous life. Being a big family, there was a very rigid routine. Eddie's grandparents were horrified. This was not at all the sort of life they wanted for their grandson and this created an enormous amount of tension between them and the foster parents. Eddie, by contrast, became very attached to his foster mother and was reluctant to be separated from her, even for short periods. His foster mother was subtly critical of Eddie's family and reluctant to encourage links. She felt that she was giving him the love that he had not hitherto experienced.

Eddie remained in the foster family for just over two years, until he was eleven. Then, partly because of pressure from his family, he was moved to a new foster family. Sam and Jenny had one daughter, Beatrice, aged six, of their own and no other children. They were unable to have any more and so had decided to adopt. Sam was a university researcher, with a public school background. Jenny was not working but had been in the theatre and was undertaking an art degree course, part-time. Certainly the environment was far more in keeping with Eddie's birth background. Eddie was very reluctant to leave his foster home and missed his foster mother terribly. At first he was unresponsive and showed some obsessive behaviour, demonstrating considerable instability. He became preoccupied with time zones across the world, having been given a very elaborate watch by a maternal aunt. He never referred to his natural mother, but made frequent references to his previous foster mother, demanding to be allowed to phone her all the time. His new school was a disaster. He made no friends and was very withdrawn. His teachers described him as 'odd'.

Eddie seemed to have an ability to make adults feel they were surplus to his requirements, in an emotional sense. Yet, by contrast, he had few skills when it came to caring for himself physically and had absolutely no ability to play creatively.

Beatrice was a much cherished child, who had been accustomed to being the focus of a great deal of attention, and was very stimulated and therefore somewhat precocious as a result. Initially, she was excited at the concept of having a new, older brother but his lack of response to her she found confusing and she also resented the amount of time and concern her parents seemed to be focusing on Eddie. She began to be disruptive at school and to under-achieve in just about every aspect of her life, which proved to be of enormous concern to her parents. Jenny began to feel hostility towards Eddie building up, because he was causing Beatrice to regress, and become so obviously unhappy.

Both Jenny and Sam were resentful towards the Social Services for not having been more open about the extent of Eddie's difficulties. In fairness to the Social Services, it was only when Eddie was removed from his initial foster family that these difficulties became apparent. Of course this was no consolation to Jenny and Sam.

Eventually the placement broke down and at the time

of writing, Eddie is now in a children's home, which is the very last place he should be.

It is clear to see from the above story that the Social Services made the mistake of too slavishly trying to re-create Eddie's birth background, no doubt because of the pressure being brought to bear by the grandparents. We do not choose the families we are born into and we will have all had the experience of knowing families where the children and parents seem to be ill-matched. Certainly, in theory, it would have been ideal for Eddie if he could have entered a family where he would have received, not only much needed maternal love, but also intellectual stimulus – but then life is not ideal. He clearly had formed a close bond with his first foster mother and it certainly seems that this relationship should not have been so under-rated. She would have been prepared to keep him permanently, in fact wanted to do so.

As for Sam and Jenny, it was very easy to see why they felt they could not cope with Eddie. There is a double tragedy here for not only has Eddie lost out on having a family of his own, but Jenny and Sam have been so undermined by the experience, that they have decided not to attempt to adopt or foster again.

Eddie's story does go to demonstrate that adopting an older child is something of a lottery. You do not know until they enter your family, how their past experiences will affect their behaviour, and whether their unruly or disruptive behaviour will be a temporary aberration or a permanent feature. It is very understandable that many prospective parents feel they cannot cope with adopting an older child. If you feel, though, you might be able to, do bear in mind that if you can offer your home to an adolescent, what you are probably doing is offering a child the very last chance to make something of his life. Many of these children live in a children's home and if they do not have the benefit of a family, will go downhill from there. If you enjoy older children and if you have the stamina, there can be few more worthwhile jobs than giving an older child a chance.

10

Adopting a disabled child

I suppose it is not at all surprising that a frequent cause of parental abandonment is due to the child being disabled. Some parents reject the child at birth, other parents try to cope, and fail. Either way, it is a heartbreaking situation for all concerned, and the need for long-term families for children of varying disabilities, is considerable. I thought it would be helpful if I listed the main factors which you should consider before deciding whether you can cope with the adoption of a disabled child. These are as follows:

- The dependency levels are likely to be very high, and may become higher. Do you have (a) the patience to cope with this, and (b) the time?

- Access to services and support. You do need to have ready access to all support systems with regard to health, education and respite care. If you live in an isolated area, then caring for a disabled child can be very hard indeed.

- Consider carefully the needs and demands of other family members. Is it actually fair on your partner and other children in the family to take on responsibility for a disabled child? You can only split yourself in so many directions. You need time for all family members, and you need time for yourself. This may be something that *you* want to do, but do the whole family want to do it? It must be a family decision.

- Following on from that, you run the risk of becoming a 'disabled family'. People tend to stare at disabled children which makes you all feel 'different'. On a practical level you may find yourself having to work your activities round places which accommodate a wheelchair, and one family member may always have to be excluded from the rest of the family's activities, to care for the disabled child. As a unit, the family can start to feel they are somehow set apart.

- Bereavement – the life expectancy of the child may be significantly reduced, or it may be that the degree of dependency will ultimately become so great that the child will no longer be able to be cared for in your home, and will need to be in hospital. Either way, can you and the other members of your family, cope with the knowledge that you may well lose the child? and is it fair to put your other children through this experience?

- Do you need any specialist skills in order to be able to cope with caring for the particular disability you have in mind, and if so, how do you acquire them?

You have to be tough to adopt a disabled child. Tough

physically, because in most cases there will be a considerable amount of physical labour involved, such as lifting, carrying, pushing wheelchairs etc., etc. and you have got to live a long time! Taking on a disabled child is taking on a child for life. Unless his disability is relatively minor, the chances are that he will not be able to make an independent home of his own. You have to consider that when most couples are enjoying retirement, you and your partner will still be in the throws of parenthood. You certainly cannot afford to be frail yourself, or have any form of recurring or persistent ill health. You also have to be mentally tough, because you are going to have to fight for your child – fight to obtain the right sort of care, fight to obtain the right sort of schooling, fight to obtain the allowances which are yours or his by right. You would think that health and local authorities would be bending over backwards to help you, bearing in mind that you are caring for a disabled child, who would cost hundreds of thousands of pounds if left in local authority care. Not so. To get what you feel your child needs will be one long battle, and you will need great tenacity to push through what you know is best for your child. You obviously have to be emotionally tough as well to cope with other people who can be so unkind, and say such horrible things. And to cope with your own feelings which from time to time will be very hard to handle. None of us are saints and sometimes the job will seem so dispiriting, such hard work and with so little reward. At other times the rewards will be so great, but, for all that, the more emotionally demanding. You will be absolutely exhausted unless you can learn to handle your feelings.

As to practical help, if you are taking on a disabled child, there are usually adoption allowances available and in some instances, the local authority will pay travelling expenses if you regularly have to attend hospital appointments. The local authority will also offer respite care, so that for several weeks of the year your child will be looked after by someone else, so that you can have a holiday or at least a rest.

Because caring for a disabled child is so taxing, many foster carers, sometimes adoptive parents, too, specialize in a particular kind of disability. This way they are able to build up skills in handling the children in their care, for the maximum benefit to the children and themselves.

> *My husband's cousin, Rita, fosters disabled children. Her speciality is caring for severely disabled newborn babies, who have been rejected by their parents at birth. Obviously in some instances, parents react in shock and horror as to what has happened, and then in a few weeks or months time, they come to terms with their baby and want to care for him themselves. Rita's job is to provide that interim care while social workers try to help the parents to decide what they want to do in the long term.*
>
> *Some of the children she has taken on have been chronically disabled, one or two have died. It is a very specialist skill to be able to cope with this sort of thing and thank heavens there are some Rita's about.*

Rita, though, can at least have a gap between children. Adopting a disabled child permanently is another matter entirely. You must consider whether you will feel trapped by the experience. Respite care is all very well, but it does not happen very often or for very long. Do you have extended family or good friends, who would enable you to sometimes get out, even if it is only for a walk in the park, or to do some shopping on your own? Of course your child may be receiving day care, or going to school, in which case this may provide the necessary break. Adopting a child needs a great deal of thought, if you are taking into your home a disabled child, that thought process needs to be all the more detailed, to make sure that everyone involved can cope.

David's story, as told by his adoptive mother, Sarah, is a nice way to end this chapter.

> *We adopted David when he was two years old. He had cerebral-palsy and had been through a rough time. Initially his mother, who was a single parent, thought she could cope with him and then decided that she could not. David went into foster care and had just settled down when his mother changed her mind again. There then followed another period with his mother, which this time went badly wrong. She developed a drink problem and David was severely neglected, so he had to go back into care. We were very nervous about meeting him, very unsure as to whether we could cope. Yet from the moment we first set eyes on him, we loved him. Although we had absolutely no experience of disabled children, his disabilities just never seemed to matter, and our doubts flew out of the window. We just wanted to love him and care for him.*
>
> *The most poignant moment of his childhood came about six years later. He had been a little pensive for a day or two, quite unlike himself. I asked him what the matter was and he said, suddenly, 'When you adopted me, did you know I would never be able to walk?'*
>
> *My husband and I couldn't bear it. 'Of course we did,' we told him.*
>
> *'We love you just the way you are.'*
>
> *He was so relieved. It was so stupid of us – it was something we should have thought of. We had told him all about being adopted, of course, but it had just never occurred to us that he might think we had not been*

aware of his disabilities. Since then, he has continued to blossom and flourish. He is a son any parent would be proud of.

11

Adopting a family group

There is quite a lot to be said for adopting a ready-made family, assuming that is, you have a robust constitution, the patience of Job and a well developed instinct for survival. Let us look at some of the main advantages:

- The whole process of adoption is fraught – the invasion of privacy, the endless interviews, the excruciating stress associated with whether or not you will be allowed to proceed, the terror of the court hearings in case anything goes wrong ... At least if you are adopting a ready-made family, you will only have to go through the system once. Although this may seem rather a superficial advantage, believe me, once faced with adoption procedure yourself, you will appreciate what I am saying.

- There are less couples prepared to take sibling groups than single children, and assuming you are approved for several children, then the chances are you are more likely to be given a placement.

- As with disabled children, sibling groups tend to attract adoption allowances. The local authority may well be prepared to spend quite large sums of money to make your home suitable and provide you with the necessary equipment to cope with multiple children.

- From the children's point of view, there are obviously enormous benefits – an enhanced sense of belonging, far less of an identity crisis than they would have if they had been adopted alone, and hopefully no individual sense of rejection: their parents could not cope with any of them.

- When interviewing families who have adopted multiple children, I found they all seemed to say the same thing – rather like undiagnosed twins born to unsuspecting parents – after the initial shock, the rewards are enormous and life is much fuller and richer than it would have been otherwise.

Equally, of course, there are distinct drawbacks:

- You have so many relationships to establish. How will you ever get to know each of the children individually? Finding time to be alone with each child can be very difficult, unless the children are well spaced in age.

- As well as having to cope with several sets of relationships, there is the question of the relationship the children have with one another. Often they will not have been with the same foster carers or in the same children's home, so they may not know each other very well. Nonetheless, there will be old scores to settle. Usually when there are several children in a family, there is someone who carries guilt about what has happened to them and someone else to carry the blame. You cannot simply wade in on these very intimate problems and start throwing your weight about. First you have to understand them and that takes time and a great deal of patience.

- It goes without saying that the workload of several children is enormous – the clothes, the food, making sure the homework is done, cubs, brownies, swimming lessons, etc., etc. Finding a moment for yourself, or with your partner, will require a military-style operation. Is the relationship between you and your partner solid enough to cope with this?

- The Agency will expect one of you not to work, or at least to work very part-time for several years, while the children settle into their new home. It could be that you have a job which fits in, like teaching, assuming the children are all of school age. Even so, your social worker will be very aware of the energy reserve you will need and it is questionable whether anyone can cope with a job, on top of settling in a ready-made family.

- One child to some extent will fit in with your lifestyle. Several children change everything. For example you may have been used to having a fortnight's package holiday in the sun each year. Chances are you will be able to afford to continue this with one child. If you suddenly acquire three children, it is fairly unlikely that the family finances will run to a holiday in the sun for all five of you. Instead, you probably will find yourself camping in the Lake District or self-catering in Cornwall, or whatever. With one child on Sunday mornings, you might persuade him to watch a video while you have a lie-in in bed with the Sunday papers, like you used to do. There is no hope of achieving this with two or three children. Someone will always be wanting your attention or fighting with their sibling. One child might well be allocated a corner of the sitting room in which to keep his toys. OK, sometimes the sitting room would look a bit of a mess but essentially at bedtime the toys could be tidied away, and your sitting room returned to normal, to entertain your friends. Forget it, if you have several children, they will take over your house. You can go through the motions of calling the kitchen, the kitchen, the sitting room, the sitting room but essentially every room in the house will be a playroom, because several children do not all want to play the same things at the same time. They need their individual space. Someone will set up some Lego in the hallway, somebody else will sort out her dolls house in the sitting room, somebody else will decide to clean his bike all over the kitchen floor. Unless you are blessed with a large house, you simply have to let multiple children go into every nook and cranny in your home, in order to provide them with the space they need.

- When you have several children, you always have an ongoing problem of some sort. It is very rare indeed if everybody is free from bugs, everybody is doing well at school, everyone is getting on with their peers, everyone is sleeping through the night etc., etc. We find with our two boys that they take it in turns to be horrors. One is a goody-goody for a few months, while the other one plays the part of the more disruptive element and then they swap. This also seems to apply to sleeping through the night. With three small children, it is rare that we have a totally undisturbed night. I am writing this book in January, which I appreciate is a bad month, but so far this year, we have had one set of tonsils extracted, three sets of chicken pox, one chest infection and two ear infections – and we lead a very healthy, outdoor life in the country with everyone taking their vitamins! In other words, if you want problem-free parenting, do not go in for multiple children.

Let us look at the story of Samuel, Sadie and Sonia, who are not untypical of the sort of family group who become available for adoption.

At the time they were adopted Samuel was eight, Sadie six and Sonia three-and-a-half. Their background was very chaotic. Their mother, Julie, was a single woman. She had been in care herself and very unhappily fostered. She maintained that she had been the subject of sexual abuse by her foster father, and certainly this seems likely. Julie became pregnant at sixteen-and-a-half, and was placed in a mother and baby hostel, where she gave birth to Samuel. Initially she considered adoption for Samuel but eventually was given a one-bedroomed local authority flat. Julie is a likeable person but of fairly low intelligence and has very poor parenting skills. In fairness she had no model from her own childhood to draw on. She was also very promiscuous and there were a series of pregnancies, some of which were terminated. Two further children, however, were born – Sadie two years after Samuel, and Sonia, two-and-a-half years after Sadie.

Julie seemed to settle into a pattern of problems – debts would accumulate, fuel would be disconnected, the children would go hungry and be neglected and then they would be bailed out and would start again. There were always different men around the flat and because of her fairly outrageous behaviour, Julie became ostracized by neighbours and frequently had to be re-housed for this reason alone. During the period of the children's early years, there was a high level of social monitoring but even so, on one occasion Sonia had to be admitted to hospital, due to failure to thrive. The crunch came one day when Julie simply disappeared after a party, having persuaded a neighbour to care for the children overnight. Despite appeals, she did not reappear and the children were the subject of a 'place of safety' order and were put into foster care. When Julie eventually reappeared, there was an attempt to rehabilitate the children with her, but it did not work and so the children were placed in two separate foster homes – Sonia on her own, and Sadie and Samuel together. Sonia instantly became very attached to her foster parents, who sought to adopt her but the decision was made that the children should remain together. Eventually, after about a year, a couple were found to adopt them – Jack in his early forties, a security officer, and Sue, a part-time secretary. They had two children of their own – a son of nineteen, who was living away from home with a girlfriend, and a daughter, of fifteen, doing GCSEs. The three children reacted very differently to their new parents. Samuel seemed easy initially, but gradually became quite babyish in his behaviour – soiling and wetting during daytime, as well as night-time and then becoming aggressive and disobedient. Sue and Jack realized that this was his need to reflect the anger he felt at the series of rejections in his life, but he was certainly not an easy child.

Sadie, by contrast, was too good. In her own mind, clearly, she had taken on the guilt for the troubles she and her siblings had suffered. She imagined it was her bad behaviour which had caused all the trouble, and she used all her energies to maintain a façade of goodness, which left her little energy to invest in relationships. Jack and Sue had to work very hard at getting her to see that it was OK to be naughty sometimes, to let go, to relax, and gradually as the months went by, she became noisier and more challenging.

Sonia, in a way, was the most difficult because she was the most heart-breaking. She was very cold and unresponsive, clearly lacking any trust after, as she saw it, being let down by a series of mothers. The bond she had formed with her foster mother was considerable and she was very depressed at having lost her. She withdrew physically and for some months refused to respond with any enthusiasm to those around her. While it was clear that Samuel and Sadie had quite a close bond, neither of them seemed very interested in Sonia, nor she in them. Jack and Sue believe that it would have been better for Sonia to have stayed with her foster carers and to have been adopted by them, which is what they and she wanted. The misery that she has suffered does not seem to be justified by the advantages of being with her siblings. The strain on Jack and Sue, trying to weld together their little family, was considerable. Sue had to give up her part-time job and both, at times, felt inadequate and close to being unable to cope.

Two years on, things are much better. The children have settled down and although Samuel still has educational problems, the girls are doing very well at school, and all three children have developed good friendships and a loving, demonstrative relationship with their parents. Jack and Sue are adamant that it was worth it, but they are the first to admit that they are not sure that they would have had the courage to undertake the adoption of all three children, had they known the problems that were in store.

If you are trying to draw any conclusions from this story, I think you might be inclined to agree with Sue and Jack that maybe Sonia should have been left where she was – in which case, Jack and Sue would have been able to give Samuel and Sadie much more attention. It does seem that they bit off more than they could chew. Maybe it was unrealistic of Sue to think that she could continue working, and of the Social Services for allowing her to try. In addition, although Jack and Sue's previous experience of parenting must have been very helpful, it may also have had the effect of making them believe that things were going to be easier than in fact they were.

By contrast, here is a story of another three not unsimilar children, in terms of family profile, which worked wonderfully well.

Katie was five, Steven four and Holly two, when they were adopted. Their parents had been married and their father was in the Army. Katie and Steven were born while the family was posted in Germany. On returning to the UK, the parents separated for a while and were then reunited in what was a very stormy relationship. As a result of their reconciliation, Holly was born, but shortly after her birth, the marital difficulties re-emerged. The father was drinking very heavily and was violent, both to his wife and children. He indulged in a series of affairs and the family were always heavily in debt. On one occasion, Steven was hit quite seriously by his father and the police were called. As a result the children were put on the child protection register.

The children's mother became increasingly depressed and lethargic, to the point where she said she could not cope with the children any more and they were removed and put in a foster home. The parents separated and the mother simply disappeared off the face of the earth. Their father, in a series of abusive interviews with the Social Services department, demanded his children back but there was no question of him having them – he was violent and unstable. When eventually their mother was traced, she said she did not wish to see them again and would like them to be placed for adoption.

The children were found a home with Martin, forty-one and Sheila, aged forty. Martin is an artist, privately educated – a mild, gentle man. For him it was a first marriage. Sheila had been married before. During her first marriage she had suffered a series of miscarriages, although it had not been understood why her pregnancies never went full term. Because there was some doubt as to whether in fact Sheila might ever have a child, the Social Services Department asked Sheila and Martin to make a commitment to use contraception, for clearly a new baby would not be appropriate if they were adopting Katie, Steven and Holly. Sheila's job was as a hospital administrator and she gave up work immediately they were approved for adoption of the children. Having several younger brothers and sisters and having been involved in hospital work, Sheila felt relatively experienced in the handling of children. Martin had nannied for two nieces when he was younger, and as he worked from home they decided they would have plenty of time between them to care for the children.

This perhaps may be the main difference between Martin and Sheila and Jack and Sue. Jack and Sue had other commitments – their jobs and their own children.

Martin and Sheila decided even before the children came to live with them, that they were going to be totally single-minded in making a success of their new family.

The main difficulty with Katie was that she had assumed the mothering role with Steven and Holly, and found it hard to relinquish control and responsibility to her new parents. She was very resistant initially to physical contact and never asked for any help, even though it was obvious that she needed it.

Steven settled in wonderfully well right from the beginning. He formed a very close attachment with Martin, and by very good fortune showed an enormous interest in drawing. The two spent many happy hours playing around in Martin's studio. Holly had some development delays and very poor speech which clearly was the result of her poor early parenting. Literally within weeks of her being in her new family, she had come on with leaps and bounds. A lively, inquisitive child, she was adored by everyone.

Within just a few months, Katie had settled down. Sheila found that by involving her in domestic decisions she was able to continue to make her feel that she had some responsibility and as the months went by, Katie started to shun this responsibility and settle more and more happily into the role of proper childhood with few responsibilities.

Both Martin and Sheila say they cannot believe how sterile and selfish their lives must have been before the children. They do not believe that any children by birth could have brought them more joy than their three adopted ones. Their friends think they are wonderful, taking on such a big responsibility, but Martin and Sheila see it the other way round – they think they are incredibly lucky.

It is very clear from these stories that if you are considering taking on a ready-made family, you must research, carefully, the problems you are likely to meet, to firmly remove the rose-tinted glasses and look at all the practical issues. Having said that, it is wonderful to be able to offer a home to a little family who might otherwise be separated, and the rewards are many.

12

Inter-racial adoption

Transracial adoption has had a fairly high press recently. Back in the sixties and seventies it was perfectly acceptable for a white couple to adopt a black child, but in recent years this practice has been stopped and there are some fairly powerful arguments for and against the decision. People of black or mixed-race parentage maintain that the only reason white people started adopting black babies in the first place, was because the supply of white babies was drying up. They say that those children adopted by white families have had real problems – they may be black on the outside but on the inside they have been brought up white, and the conflicting identity crisis has caused them no end of difficulty.

Undoubtedly there is a considerable amount of evidence to support this view, yet the argument for inter-racial adoption also has its merits. Which is best for a child – to be brought up in a children's home, to be shifted from one foster family to the next, or to be brought up in the stability of a family, albeit a white family, and to be given a loving and secure childhood?

> *Alan and I attended an adoption meeting at our local Social Services about three years ago, just prior to our going to Romania to adopt Michael. The then acting Head of Adoption/Fostering, told us that there were sixty children available in the area for adoption, but forty of them were of mixed race, or black. There were fourteen couples, including ourselves, at the meeting and we were all white. So that meant that as far as the forty children were concerned, no adoptions were going to be possible as a result of that meeting.*

The attitude to inter-racial adoption varies enormously from local authority to local authority. Some are absolutely adamant that no black or mixed-race child should be adopted by white parents. Others take a different view. They try very hard to find a racially appropriate family but if they cannot, then they are prepared to consider a white family, to give a child the opportunity of family life which otherwise would be denied to him. In addition, they try to find families who have some sort of link with the child's culture. Maybe the adoptive parents teach in a school which contains a good mix of black children, maybe they live in a mixed-race area, maybe they have friends of mixed race – some link, in other words. Certainly one can see that a black child brought up in a middle-class white family, in an area where there is not a black face to be seen, smacks of trouble.

Instinctively one feels increasingly this is an issue which needs to be addressed. As our culture becomes more and more transracial, there are presumably going to be an increasing number of children of mixed race. While it is important to give the children a sense of cultural identity, I think it is also important to try and look to the future when one would like to think that the colour of a person's skin is no more important than the colour of their hair.

There are a number of black children in the UK who are the result of inter-country adoption. In the past, places such as Sri Lanka, Brazil, Mexico, India, have all been places favoured by European couples seeking to adopt a baby. Adopting a child from these countries is expensive and so by definition the couples who adopt, tend to fall into this much criticized category of middle class and affluent. Certainly it would be dangerous to fall into the trap of believing that a delightful little coffee coloured baby will grow up without any anger or resentment or confusion, about his origins and the colour of his skin. And the problems will begin quite soon ... once a child goes to school, inevitably he will have to cope with taunts. It is very difficult for a white family, who will have had little or no experience of colour prejudice, to understand what their son or daughter is going through – and to know how to help them. If you find yourself in this position, the starting point has to be to try and imagine what it is like to be a black child, growing up in still a predominantly white country. Despite all the attempts to avoid colour prejudice, if you think of the average television programme, book, advertisement, film ... they are still predominantly white. I am not saying this is necessarily wrong, but it does make it difficult for the black child. Without force-feeding your child on black culture, you can do a lot to help him be proud of who he is. Make sure your home contains pictures and posters which reflect your child's country of origin. Make sure you have black dolls and books featuring black children, videos too, and above all make sure that your child has some black friends, even if it means going out of your area to find them.

Here is the story of one little black boy who was adopted in unusual circumstances.

David is the youngest of seven children. His mother, Lorraine, is white and her seven children are by three different fathers. David's father, Jeff, is a West Indian, and all Lorraine's other children are white. The two eldest are young adults and a third and fourth child are in residential care.

Lorraine's lifestyle was very chaotic and she had a history of poor parenting skills. Around the time of her association with David's father, she became an alcoholic and needed a great deal of Social Services support. All the children were placed on the care and protection register, as a consequence of general neglect.

Shortly after David was born, one of his elder siblings was involved in an incident where his arm was badly burnt on the cooker. Nonetheless, Lorraine's apparent good nature and good intentions towards the children seduced social workers into leaving the children at home. However when David was eighteen months old, he fell out of an upstairs window and this incident led to all the remaining children being placed in care. David, who was failing to thrive, was placed on his own with very experienced short-term carers. Lorraine showed no interest in having her children back and in any event, within three months of them being taken into care, she sadly died as a result of stomach cancer.

Nine months later David was placed for adoption with a single white woman, with a seven-year-old daughter by a Trinidadian father. The single woman's name is Sarah and she works part-time as a dental nurse. The decision on the face of it seems rather an unusual one, but in fact Sarah is in many respects ideal. Her daughter was thrilled with her new little brother and Sarah, with many black friends, was able to provide both children with plenty of contact with the black *community. Sarah's main problem strangely enough was not with the children at all – David settled in extremely well and as a little family unit, they bonded very quickly. The problem lay with Sarah's mother. Sarah was an only child of a middle-class family. Her parents were naturally very shocked when Sarah had a baby born illegitimately to a black father, who deserted them before the birth. Initially they would have nothing to do with her, but when Sarah's father died, Sarah's mother, Rosemary, turned more and more to her daughter and in fact had become extremely fond of her granddaughter. In turn, Rosemary acted as a very good support system for Sarah in helping her cope as a single parent. When Sarah adopted David, Rosemary saw it as capitalizing on one mistake by making another. Sarah was furious. She felt sure that if she had adopted a white child, it would have been perfectly acceptable to her mother and saw her mother's prejudice towards David as being a reflection not only on David but also on Rosemary. For a while things were very difficult, and it looked as though mother and daughter would lose touch again. However, Sarah's natural warmth and the fact that she was making such a success of parenthood won her mother round. Rosemary is now an excellent grandmother to both children.*

The case of Sarah and David is interesting. Obviously it is more difficult to adopt a child if you are single, and it is probably accurate to say that if Sarah's daughter had been white as opposed to mixed race, Sarah might never have been able to adopt a child at all. As it is, her connection with the black community made it possible for her to be considered for David.

It is difficult to see how you could 'manufacture' a

situation for yourself whereby you could be considered for a black child, as a white person. If you naturally associate socially with black families or live in a mixed-race area, then you may well be considered. It is doubtful, however, that if you rushed out to steep yourself in black culture, you would necessarily be considered for a black child. One can but hope that as years go by, the definition between different cultures in this country becomes more blurred and the rules less strict. However you look at it, it still seems terrible to me that children should be living in institutions when there are loving families only too happy to give them a home but are prevented from doing so, because of the colour of their skin.

13

Adopting a sexually abused child

Despite the fact that sexual abuse gets quite an airing in the press, it is still, for many people, a taboo subject. So horrific is the concept of sexually abusing a small child that it is easier to pretend it does not really happen. It is hard to tell whether as a crime it is on the increase, brought on by hard porn videos and magazines, or whether it is simply a crime which has always been there, but only recently has received sufficient exposure.

The loss of a child's innocence is so fundamental, it is hard to imagine that any child – particularly a child who has been abused over a prolonged period – can ever regain the magic of childhood. What makes the experience so particularly damaging is that usually the perpetrator of the crime is the very person who the child should be able to trust implicitly – ie., a parent or a very close relation.

While many sexually abused children find the whole experience both terrifying and painful, while most of them are aware that what is happening is wrong, the fact is that the abuse they receive may be the only form of love in their otherwise miserable lives. When a child is removed from her family it is all too easy to assume that she will have a sense of relief. In fact it is equally likely that she will suffer a profound sense of loss. As she grows and matures, of course, the realization of how wrongly she was treated may build up a sense of loathing for the abuser. However, initially the small child may well miss the perpetrator, whether a parent or a family friend, very much indeed.

So how do you face the prospect of adopting a child who you know has been sexually abused? Is this knowledge going to loom as a big thing in all your lives, or is it something that you feel you can deal with, and gradually help the child to regain her lost childhood?

One of the most important aspects of dealing with a sexually abused child is not to judge or be critical of your child's parents – *even the abuser*. When discussing the child's experiences, try to explain, as gently as possible, that there are different kinds of love – the way Mummy's and Daddy's love each other and the way children and parents love each other. In her case, Daddy had simply got things muddled up and loved her in the wrong sort of way. It will be hard to adopt this attitude when probably all your instincts scream to tear this man who has made your little child suffer so much, apart, but it is vitally important that you do not condemn.

I thought perhaps the best way to highlight what you are up against is to describe an actual case of abuse and list the problems faced by the adoptive couple.

> *Hayley was put up for adoption at the age of seven. Her mother was an alcoholic and it was for this reason that Hayley was admitted into care. However, while in her foster family, Hayley admitted to her foster mother that her mother's co-habitee had sexually abused her, for at*

least two years. Certainly doctors were able to confirm that Hayley had been seriously abused over what appeared to be a long period.

There was no question of Hayley going back to her mother, since she was not prepared to give up her relationship with her co-habitee and so Hayley was put up for adoption. She was placed nine months later with Derek, an insurance agent, aged thirty-six, and Maureen, a chef of thirty-three, who gave up her job to care for Hayley. Derek and Maureen have one son, by birth, of four but were unable to have any more natural children, due to Maureen having undergone an early hysterectomy.

These are the main problems which Derek and Maureen faced:

- *From the time Hayley first arrived, she tried to imitate any physical contact between Maureen and Derek, with strong, sexual overtones. She quite literally made overtures towards Derek of a quite sexual nature. Derek found this very hard to handle. On the one hand, he was desperately anxious to compensate for Hayley's absence of a warm, affectionate father figure in her life. At the same time he found her behaviour embarrassing and awkward. Maureen, much to her astonishment, found that she became quite jealous of Hayley's behaviour towards Derek, and this in turn caused a great deal of tension between everyone. They recognized it was a question of trying to teach Hayley to achieve spontaneous contact without causing everyone discomfort, but it was not easy.*

- *Hayley suffered from a very poor self-image. As far*

as she was concerned, the only time she was appreciated was when she was being abused by her mother's co-habitee. The concept that she might be liked for herself was an anathema, which was why it was terribly important that neither Derek nor Maureen reacted angrily when her overtures to Derek were inappropriate. Recognizing the problem and being able to handle it, of course, were two different things.

- *Hayley was angry at being separated from her mother and her mother's lover. There was a great deal of anger to come out of her and most of it was directed at Maureen.*

- *Derek and Maureen's son, Matthew, also became involved in sexualized play as a result of Hayley's approaches to him. This shocked and horrified Derek and Maureen. They could not help resenting Hayley for exposing Matthew to this and were desperate to protect their child.*

- *Hayley absorbed a disproportionate amount of parental time, which Matthew found very hard to handle. In a way it almost seemed as though as the weeks went by, Hayley thrived, while Matthew withdrew into himself. This again put a tremendous strain on Maureen and Derek's relationship with Hayley.*

- *The horror of sexual abuse did affect the domestic atmosphere of the home. There were a great many unfamiliar and unhelpful emotions about – confusion, fear, sadness, guilt, grief, disbelief. Maureen and Derek's well ordered life was thrown up into the air. They were no longer dealing with the ordinary but the extra-ordinary and they found that very hard.*

Two years on, Derek and Maureen feel that they have made it. They have gradually exchanged Hayley's inappropriate behaviour for something acceptable, without rejecting her physical advances. Her relationship with Matthew has improved enormously and they do now play, well and normally together. Derek and Maureen are aware that problems are likely to re-emerge when Hayley reaches adolescence. The onset of her periods or her first sexual encounter, may well bring back all that she suffered as a little girl, and she may need a great deal of help to move into happy, settled adulthood. Nonetheless, despite the tough times, they feel that it has worked and that they have had enough of her childhood to really put things right for her, to give her stability before she has to face adult life for real. Both Derek and Maureen are not sure that they would have been able to achieve this had Hayley come to them any older, and they both say that although they had received extensive counselling before Hayley arrived, nothing had prepared them for the inappropriateness of her behaviour, nor the enormous amount of anger she felt at what had happened to her.

It is difficult to separate an abused child from what has happened to her in one's mind. As a nation we are not good at discussing feelings, particularly of a sexual nature, yet communication is absolutely vital. If the child in your care is to recover from her experiences, then she must be able to talk them through, as often and for as long as she wants.

SECTION 3

Living with adoption

14

Inter-country adoption

It is hard to know where to begin, for inter-country adoption is such a muddle at the moment. Increasingly since the 1970s, childless couples have been looking at countries abroad from which to adopt, when they find they are not eligible for a baby here in the UK. Their stories follow a familiar pattern – years of infertility treatment which ultimately proves fruitless, and then a discussion with the Social Services which makes them realize that either they will not be considered for adoption at all, or that if they are, it will be for a much older child.

In the past many children have been adopted from South American countries – from Brazil, Chile, Columbia. For a while Sri Lanka was very popular, also Peru, Thailand, El Salvador, Hong Kong, India ... Then, on Christmas Day, 1989, a mad dictator named Nicolae Ceausescu was shot dead and within a few weeks the world learnt of the orphanages of Romania. Suddenly adopting a child from abroad was not something that just childless couples did in desperation. For many families it seemed morally right to give a child who would otherwise live and die in an institution, the chance of a loving family and, in many cases, life itself. Like us, they boarded the Tarom flights to Bucharest and struggled with the nightmare that followed, and it is the Romanian orphanage children who have been responsible for the current debate on inter-country adoption.

Emotions run very high on the subject. There are people who believe we are all citizens of the World and that while children suffer, families who can give them a home – a loving home – should do so. Then there is the lobby which says that no child should be taken from its cultural heritage. For parents who have experienced the horrors of orphanages around the world, with all the terrible suffering, this argument is insane. What cultural heritage is there for a child lying in a stinking cot, malnourished, unloved, day-after-day, month-after-month, year-after-year until he dies or goes mad?

I have just dropped Michael, our Romanian born son, off at school before coming to work this morning, to write this chapter. He ran ahead of me into his classroom, clutching a Sainsbury's carrier bag full of dinosaurs – the current school project. He was hailed by half a dozen of his classmates, his teacher gave him a hug. I was summarily dismissed and as I left, there he was, head bent over a desk, chattering away with a group of friends – strong, healthy, articulate and well balanced. The hair that had once been a matted, grey stubble was now a rich, glossy chestnut, the hands that he could only use as shovels can now deftly work on a puzzle ... *and all this in two years*. If Michael had not been adopted, he would be dead and what use would his cultural heritage have been to him then?

But enough philosophizing – the decision as to whether you feel you can adopt a child from another country, another culture, perhaps of another colour, is one that only you and your partner can make. What is essential is that you must recognize that if you are going to adopt a child from another country, you will be also adopting that country. You must be sure to build up the child's sense of pride in where he came from, to acquire as much information as you can about his family, his background and, when possible and appropriate, visit the country, teach the child his native language and keep the link going. Then, once the child is grown he is in a position to make his own decision. He will hold a British passport, he will be a British citizen, he can embrace the country that raised him and give little thought to his origins. Alternatively, he can turn his back on Britain, say thank you very much and go back to where he came from, but at least he will be strong and healthy in mind and body, with the experience of loving and being loved behind him. It is all we can do for any of our children. If we are adopting a child, particularly a child from another country, then all that is really required of us is to slightly widen the options available so that the child has a choice – to go/to stay/to keep a foot in each camp.

Equally though, I think it is important not to make a child feel too different. The last thing a child can bear is to be the odd man out. For example if you and your family are Church of England, if your child is going to go to a C of E school, then although in theory raising him as a Muslim or in the Orthodox Church, or whatever, is appropriate for his origins and might seem like a nice gesture, it will also make him stand out from his peers, which he will hate. You have to raise your child as just that – *your child*. He will have to take on board your culture, and provided you make sure he has access to, and is aware of, the culture of his country of birth, in my view you have done your duty.

THE PROCEDURE FOR ADOPTING A CHILD FROM ABROAD

In theory at some time in the future, legislation is going to be brought in to standardize the procedure for the adoption of children from abroad, and bring it into line so that it is much the same as for adoption in this country. However, as I said at the beginning of this chapter, at the moment it is a mess. Assuming you have decided you want to adopt a child from abroad, your starting point is to contact either your Social Services or a recognized agency, and ask them to undertake a home study. Before you embark on the home study, however, you have to decide which country you wish to adopt from, for the home study cannot be undertaken for a non-specific country. There are various organizations who can give you advice as to which country to go to and these are listed at the back of this book. The Government has also set up a help line for inter-country adoption, although I have to say our experiences of it are not encouraging – we seemed to know more than they did! So, first decide on your country and it is no good being even slightly non-specific. For example, we had permission to adopt a second child from Romania but when the doors closed, we decided to try and adopt from Bulgaria instead. Although the two countries are in Eastern Europe, lie cheek by jowl and have an almost identical history and culture, we had to go right through the whole process again. So it is no good thinking in terms of Eastern Europe or South America, you have to be quite specific. As well as talking to the various help organizations such as STORK (listed at the back of the book), you could also contact the Embassy of the country from which you are hoping to adopt, who should be able to give you information as to how to proceed. By far the best way of establishing how to adopt from a specific country is to find a couple who have already done so. Not only will they be able to fill you in on all the pitfalls and problems, but they will be able to give you that most valuable of all things, CONTACTS – the lawyer who is honest, the taxi driver who speaks the language and does not rip you off, the right place to stay, etc., etc.

Unlike applying to adopt a child from the UK, the completion of the home study itself may not be all that simple. Some local authorities are very opposed to the concept of inter-country adoption and therefore the social workers are reluctant to undertake home studies, saying that they have better things to do and have their work cut our caring for the children in this country. By law, they cannot refuse you a home study but, of course, how easy they make it and how long they take to do it is in their hands. There may well be a charge – those authorities who are in favour of inter-country adoption may undertake a home study for free or for a low fee, but some Social Services have been known to charge as much as two and a half thousand pounds. This, of course, is all grossly unfair but it is how the system works at the moment. Alternatively, there are several approved agencies who will undertake a home study, which will be acceptable to the local authority. Here again, of course, a fee will be charged. As a rule of thumb six hundred pounds should be about right.

The requirement of each country varies considerably. All countries require confirmation that you have no police record, which forms part of the home study anyway. Most countries require some sort of indication as to your income and financial stability. All countries require a medical report, which again forms part of the home study. Essentially what you will be trying to do is to assemble a file, having established from a self-help group or from the Embassy what that file should contain. You should also add common-sense information – photographs of your home and of your other children. If you have adopted a child before, whether from abroad or the UK, then before and after photographs to show how he or she has flourished will be helpful. All documents being presented need to be notarized and legalized. Notarized means taking the documents to a Notary Public, legalized means taking them to the Foreign Office in Petty France, London, for stamping. In addition, some countries will require the file to be stamped by their own Embassy. All this official stamping is not cheap. You can find yourself easily spending five or six hundred pounds on a complete file, but in most countries the more red ribbons and seals you seem to have, the more effective the paperwork!

When you consider the costs of travelling abroad, particularly if you are going any distance, plus accommodation, lawyers' fees etc., etc., it is obviously very important that you get your paperwork right. To travel all that way and find that you are missing vital documentation is a nightmare.

The real problem associated with producing this file is that obviously an integral part of the file is the home study. Some local authorities and most agencies will give you your home study when it is completed, others will not. Instead, one is involved in an elaborate permission procedure. First your home study is presented to the adoption panel for approval, just as if you were adopting from the UK, and then it will be sent to the Department of Health for them to give approval. The Department of Health operate as the unofficial adoption agency for inter-country adoption in this country. Most countries have proper inter-country adoption agencies whose job it is to help facilitate overseas adoptions, but in Britain we do not, as yet, and the Department of Health try to fill the gap, one has to say none too effectively. They are supposed to co-ordinate all applications because ultimately once you have found a child and are seeking to bring that child into the UK, the Home Office will need to provide you with entry clearance, and they can only do this if they are given the go ahead from the Department of Health.

This is where the whole inter-country adoption situation becomes truly ludicrous. Assuming you have done everything correctly and gone via the Department of Health route, you may ultimately receive your file back, completed and stamped. The Department of Health will *refuse* to give you the file but it may be that they will pass it directly to the Embassy of the country of your choice, and they will give you back your file. The situation with each country is different. If you are trying to adopt from Romania (which is virtually a closed book these days) you will not be given your file back at all. The Department of Health will pass it directly to the Romanian Adoption Committee.

Assuming, though, that somehow you manage to obtain your file back, with permission to proceed, then you will go to the country of your choice. Hopefully, you will find a child who is available for adoption and after a period of anything from a few days to a few months, you will be able to obtain the adoption of that child in his or her country. The child will then be legally yours but that does not mean that you can necessarily bring him into this country, legally at any rate. Assuming the country you have chosen has diplomatic relations with the UK, then in theory the British Embassy in that country, with permission from the Home Office, can stamp the child's passport with a visa to enable the child to be brought into the UK. Problems arise when either the British Embassy is extremely ineffectual, uncooperative, or non-existent, and this I have to say is all too frequently the case. I have spoken to a woman who finally adopted twin boys from Sri Lanka. Before this she had three attempts to try to adopt babies and on each occasion, while she tried desperately to do the right thing and obtain entry clearance to bring the child into the country, the child died. In the end she simply brought her two boys in without permission and in the circumstances, who can blame her for that?

There are many similar stories surrounding adoption from Romania, where parents knew that if they waited any longer, either their children would die from malnutrition and lack of care, or would contract HIV. The Government are very quick to rap the knuckles of these parents, saying they are behaving irresponsibly by breaking the rules, but what do you do? Do you watch the child that you have grown to love, who you have adopted legally in the country of his birth, die, while you wait for the good old British bureaucrats to stir the paper on their desks? We were very lucky with Michael, because we had a very sympathetic social worker, who understood the procedure of inter-country adoption well. Our adoption was very quick, but even so we had nearly nine weeks of knowing Michael, knowing of his suffering and being unable to do anything much to help him. The nightmare of those weeks is with us still.

So in selecting the country from which you are going to try and adopt, it is not so much a question of where you would *like* to go, but where you *can* go. For example, currently, there are many former USSR states who have children in pitiful conditions in orphanages. They have no hope of being rehabilitated with their parents, and because the country is so impoverished, there is no question of them being adopted by fellow countrymen. In theory, adoption in these states is quite easy. For example, until recently, a number of couples adopted children from Moldava. The problem is entry clearance. Because the former USSR is in such a shambles, individual states do not yet have diplomatic relations set up with countries abroad. Therefore the Embassy representing all the states remains in Moscow. Moldava is on the Northern Romanian border. There is absolutely no way that one could possibly arrange for a Moldavan child's passport to be stamped by Moscow, who would not know what was going on in Moldava, and in any event, would not be prepared to do it. So, your Moldavan child might well be legally yours as a result of the adoption in that country but in theory, at any rate, the child could not be brought into this country.

By contrast, at the moment there is a loophole with Turkey. Adopting children from Turkey is very easy – the whole court procedure only takes a few weeks. The Turkish authorities are very cooperative and because of some long standing diplomatic relations between Turkey and the UK, there is no requirement for entry clearance, because a Turkish adoption is recognized in this country. This is in fact ludicrous because the Turkish adoption procedure is very lax, whereas many other countries – including much of Eastern Europe – have a very good, thorough judicial process of adoption, which is not recognized by the UK – yet another discrepancy.

This brings me on to the second part of the nightmare. Assuming for a moment that you have been able to adopt your child in the child's country of birth and that somehow, whether with entry clearance or illegally, you have managed to bring the child into this country, you then usually face a whole second adoption process. This is because most countries' adoption procedure is not recognized in the UK. Once your child is in this country, for the following year you will be regularly visited by your social worker. At the end of this time she will produce yet another report, similar in fact to the home study but a sort of update on how you have all settled in and how the child is doing. Only when the child has been with you for a year, can you apply to the British court for UK adoption. It is only where the UK have quite specific agreements with particular countries that there is no need for this second adoption process and this is, at the moment, where Turkey scores. However what applies at the time of writing, I am fairly confident, will not be the case by the time this book is published.

COSTS

One of the aspects one has to consider very carefully before contemplating inter-country adoption is the costs involved. These are very restrictive, for it is an extremely expensive business. Let us look at what you can expect to have to pay. Unless your Social Services Department is particularly sympathetic to inter-country adoption, they will charge you a fee for a home study. All recognized adoption agencies naturally have to do so. The fees, depending on where you live, can range from about six hundred pounds to two and a half thousand pounds. To this you have to add the costs of notarizing and legalizing your documents, for which you should allow another five hundred pounds.

So far as the process of adoption overseas is concerned, naturally this varies enormously from country to country. Suffice to say that two thousand pounds is a fairly standard fee for a lawyer to charge for an adoption. In some cases where a child is being found for you, either through an adoption agency or via a doctor or orphanage, or indeed the lawyer himself, the procurement fee can make the overall fees rise very steeply, so that you could well find yourself paying anything up to seven thousand pounds. To this, of course, you have to add the costs of your flights (we flew to Romania four times) and your hotel accommodation or the rental of a temporary flat, and then there are the lawyer's fees back in the UK, assuming that the country you have chosen is not recognized by the UK judicial system. The fees in this country currently are about a thousand pounds, assuming that your case is not contested and there are no particular complications associated with it. You can see, therefore, there are grounds for saying that the whole exercise could well cost you between ten and fifteen thousand pounds.

So where does the future lie for inter-country adoption? The new White Paper which has been published, is proposing to make it a criminal offence to bring a child into the country without entry clearance. The lobby against inter-country adoption can easily make a case for saying this is right, that it is vital you first seek permission to bring the child into the country before doing so. I would agree with this, if there was some way in which entry clearance could be efficiently and speedily handled. It is no good trying to enforce a law, when there are no mechanics in place to facilitate doing it legally. Is it reasonable to expect anyone to watch the child they have adopted dying before their eyes, while they wait for the bureaucrats to act? What about the arguments that inter-country adoption encourages illegal baby trafficking and facilitates child pornography and, even one is told, the use of children as organ donors? Evil people abound in every society and in every country in the world. If there were no facilities for adopting from abroad, these people would simply kidnap the children, as indeed many do. As for cultural heritage, I can only repeat the argument – is it better to be alive and loved in a country other than the one in which you were born, or to be incarcerated in a loveless institution, or dead? And what about the question of too many foreigners coming into this country? Currently, there is an ever increasing imbalance in our population – not enough babies are being born to grow up and support the massive increase in elderly people. In other words, the birth rate has declined and our ability to live longer has dramatically increased. Quite simply we need more children in the country. A baby adopted from abroad is not a great cost to the national purse. Yes, there is some free schooling to consider and some free health care, but the main costs are shouldered by the parents. What cost does a continuing and agonizing childless state cause the nation? For women, in particular, the inability to have a child when one desperately wants one, can cause all sorts of problems – psychological and even physical illnesses, an inability to work and the effect on the marriage, too, can be catastrophic. Divorces are costly to the nation, whether it be Legal Aid, providing two lots of housing or the fact that the health of divorced people suffers considerably.

If one was to look at it as no more than a cost exercise, inter-country adoption would probably be of benefit to this country. After all that fuss about Romania, all that debate culminating in adoption from that country being virtually stopped, do you know how many children were brought into this country? FIVE HUNDRED! If twenty-five thousand had been brought out (and God knows there are twenty-five thousand who desperately need a home) it would not have had an enormous impact on this country. Those children would have been absorbed into loving homes, and judging by all the children that I have met, would have very quickly recovered from their ordeal. I believe their contribution to this country would be of considerable benefit.

So how does all this affect you? You can adopt a child from abroad, if you are really determined to succeed. If you feel you cannot cope with an older child and desperately want a baby, but are too old, this is the only route open to you. It is not easy and it is not cheap, but if it is what you really want to do, and either the Social Services or an adoption agency are able to provide you with a home study, then it can be done.

15

When things go right – bonding and learning to give and receive love

However awful a child's life may have been before being adopted, it is still what he has been used to. Whether he has been living in a children's home or with foster parents, whether he comes from an appallingly deprived orphanage in Eastern Europe or Asia, whether he has been used to being hit or abused, or both, he cannot simply walk away from his old life without glancing over his shoulder. There is considerable evidence to suggest that children who have been abused and beaten, often have a very strong attachment to their tormentor, for the simple reason that it may be the only attention they have received from anyone. A children's home may seem bleak and, of course, an institution is no place for a child, but the routine and familiarity do create comfort of a sort. Therefore, do not be lulled into thinking that because you have so much to offer your child when, finally, he comes to live with you he is going to be over the moon about the change in his life. Just because he has a lovely bedroom and a new bike and the promise of a seaside holiday and above all, parents at last, longing to give him care and comfort, it does not instantly put everything right.

In those early days much damage can be done by parents' high expectations of how the child will feel when suddenly confronted with such an improvement in his lifestyle. All I can ask you to do is to try and relate the child's feelings to your own experiences. Think how hard it is to adjust when we move house, or job. Think how even in the most loving of partnerships, the early days of living together can be very confusing and difficult. For a school age child, not only may he be leaving what was home but he is likely to be changing schools and losing friends as well. Maybe you can maintain some links, but maybe not, for the child may come from a completely different part of the country or even the World. With a very young child, routine has a particular value. Certainly when Michael first arrived, I maintained his orphanage routine for some weeks until gradually he settled in with Charlie. It would have been quite wrong to have changed everything in his life.

If your child has been with foster parents, then good cooperation with them can be of enormous benefit. Some foster parents can be unhelpful, particularly if they have wanted to adopt the child themselves or have strong views as to the sort of family the child should go to. If you can gain their support it is likely to make all the difference as to how your child views the forthcoming adventure. Foster parents can also give you helpful hints about the child's behaviour and how to handle her in a way that no one else can, including your social worker.

Conversely, do be careful if the child appears to adjust marvellously and immediately. It may well be a front. Children recognize that they have no control over their own lives and they simply take the philosophical view that it is better to do what is expected of them, whereas in fact they may be deeply unhappy and insecure underneath.

THE BIRTH OF LOVE FROM THE CHILD'S POINT OF VIEW

How children react to having their lives permanently sorted out will vary enormously, but whatever the circumstances and whoever they are, suddenly they will be in the spotlight. Having been children who apparently no one wanted, suddenly they are wanted very much. Expectations are running high all round – usually too high. Right from the beginning, it is terribly important to give your newly adopted child plenty of space, not to swamp him with too much affection and attention, until he has had time to adjust to his surroundings. This does not mean for a moment that you should be stand-offish or appear cold. You need to make it obvious that you want hugs and cuddles and communication, but that you are prepared to wait until he is ready to give them. Certainly I know that with the Romanian adoptions there were a number of initial problems, particularly for childless couples. If you have wanted a baby for years and finally, after months of anguish, bring home a child who by definition is enormously deprived, then the overwhelming desire has to be to smother the child with love and care. However, the Romanian children – especially those from the orphanages – had been used to being alone for twenty-three hours out of every twenty-four. Suddenly having so much attention was overwhelming and they found it hard to cope.

Love is something you have to learn to give and receive. A child who has never known love to any degree, will find the whole experience of sharing feelings with another person, of being the centre of someone else's life, both astonishing and overwhelming. It is terribly important, therefore, to take the lead from the child, to proceed with the development of your relationship at the child's pace, and above all to keep your expectations low. Instantly this removes the pressure.

It is very hard to anticipate the moment your child starts to love you because the reactions can vary so much. You may well take delivery of a very good child who, as she relaxes into her new home, with her new parents, becomes increasingly naughty. The birth of love could be doing something extremely bad, because for the first time the child knows that you love her no matter what and at last she has the confidence to be herself. The birth of love may well come when your happy-go-lucky toddler, who appears to love the world and everyone in it, becomes clingy and tearful, never wanting you for one moment out of his sight. Whenever it occurs, though, you will recognize it for what it is.

THE BIRTH OF LOVE FROM THE PARENTS' POINT OF VIEW

Parental love is different from other forms of this much discussed emotion. Parental love is uncritical and unwavering. If you have a relationship with a member of the opposite sex and he, in your view behaves badly, it affects how you view him. You might have seen him as the man you were going to marry and now, suddenly, you are not too sure, not if he can behave like that! Parental love differs in as much that it makes no difference how your child behaves. You might be disappointed or hurt, but the love does not shift, it stays in place, solid as a rock. Curiously – and, of course, this causes a good deal of trouble – it does not really alter much with the passage of the years. Parental love simply does not adjust. I read in the paper quite recently of a ninety-two-year-old woman, who rung up her seventy-one-year-old son every day to remind him to take his heart pills – *that is parental love*. It does not make a lot of difference that the recipient is an old age pensioner!

But just because it is special, and deep, and once established almost impossible to kill off, it does not mean that parental love is something that flies through the window, on the end of Cupid's arrow. Often it has to be worked at. The first time you meet your child, it is unlikely that you will be overwhelmed by love. Some deep and genuine attachment may seem to develop, certainly a commitment born of compassion and a genuine desire to help, but love may take some time. However, do not for one moment think that the love of an adopted parent is in any way inferior to the love of a birth parent because of this. There are plenty of women around who are perfectly prepared to admit that the first time they saw their newborn baby, they thought 'Yuk, take it away and let me have some sleep!' Parental love is made, not born.

One of the problems that may well confront you will be in that first meeting with the child. Over the preceding weeks or months, you will have learnt a very great deal about the child you are proposing to adopt. You will have been shown a video, given photographs and you will have learnt by heart the child's history. Then you meet in the flesh for the first time. The child may be vastly different from your expectations – the video may have been shot a few years before, the child may be obviously much older, thinner, fatter, with darker hair. The photograph you may have been staring at week in and week out, may have been that of a chubby five-year-old. Now, you are staring into the face of a lean, gaunt, knowing seven-year-old. It can be an enormous shock, so do prepare yourself for it. The other very natural thing which prospective parents do is to build up a series of daydreams in their mind. A make believe scenario of how things would be – the child will take one look at you and plead to go home with you, or the three of you will walk away into the mist, and live happily ever after. You know it is not going to be like that, your social worker has told you it is not going to be like that, but still you build up images in your mind, telling yourself that you know best, that you and this child will have an instant bond. Try to avoid doing this because it lays you open to so much hurt.

Deluding yourself can be dangerous *after* you have had that initial meeting as well. During the vital introductory period when you are visiting the child, occasionally taking him out for the day, ultimately for the weekend, try and maintain contact with your true feelings. If the relationship really is not working, so much heartache can be saved by admitting to it there and then. So somewhere along the line you have to strike a balance, between not expecting too much and therefore being instantly disappointed when things are not wonderfully right, against giving up too soon because of an unrealistic fantasy.

Margaret's experiences may help to demonstrate what is likely to be involved.

Pete and I were married for nearly eleven years before we realized we were never going to have children. By then I was thirty-six and Peter forty-one. Once we knew that there was no way we were ever going to have a baby, and after much self-searching, we contacted our local Social Services and applied to be adoptive parents of what we realized would be an older child. The whole procedure for being accepted was far more vigorous than we had anticipated and it took such a long time. They did not seem to rate us very highly, because of our lack of experience with children. I'd had a lot to do with bringing up half-siblings twelve years younger than me but apart from that, it was true – Pete and I did not even have any nieces, nephews or God-children. The other problem was that we had decided that Pete would be the main carer. Pete is a freelance artist who works from home. I am a solicitor and at the time had just been made a partner in my practice. It was clearly crazy for me to give up my career at this particular stage, whereas for Pete, it was no problem – he could just take on less work. We were both completely happy with this, but the Social Services saw it as something of a stumbling block. Eventually, though, we were approved and after what seemed an interminable wait, were matched with a little girl called Julie. Her history was sad – a very unstable, early life with her mother who had a drink problem and a series of lovers. Julie had never known who her real father was. Then she was badly beaten by one of her mother's lovers and had been taken into care. She had been in two foster homes since. The bond with her mother appeared to have been quite strong and attempts had been made to try and reconcile mother and daughter, but to no avail.

The Social Services felt that maybe Julie would fit with us, for the very reason that Pete would be the main carer. As they saw it, Julie, at nine, was not going to be prepared to accept initially a substitute mother because her attachment to her own mother was still strong, despite everything.

We began seeing her – a very pretty little girl with red

hair. She seemed to get on with Pete immediately, though with me she was much more reserved. Eventually, after many visits, she was allowed to come to live with us permanently. You could say from the very beginning things worked out well, but then you would be talking about Pete and Julie, not me. I was really pleased for them both and I honestly do not think I was jealous. The bond between them grew tangibly day-in, day-out. When we were alone Pete talked about very little else but what Julie had done during the day. He did not seem even slightly interested in me and my career any more. And Julie was so different from how I had imagined my daughter would be. I suppose you could say I am something of a feminist. I have had to work very hard to get where I am. There was no encouragement at home to go to University, and life has been a perpetual struggle. Julie, by contrast, is such a feminine little thing – she loves playing with dolls and wearing pretty dresses. I suppose I had been hoping for a daughter who would wear dungarees and take life by the short and curlies. Julie was so passive and gentle.

We had a number of rows, Pete and I. I had to be honest with him, I had to tell him that I did not love her, that I could not see I ever would. He was shocked, appalled and also I can see it now, terrified. He thought that if my feelings became known, perhaps Julie would be taken away from us. I tried to reassure him that there was no way the Social Services would make the mistake of splitting him and Julie now, but like him I was not sure. I began to question in my mind what kind of relationship Pete and I would have if due to me, Julie was taken away from us. It was not a good thought.

I do not know how things would have resolved but for the accident. Julie came out of school and busy talking, walked out from behind a parked car and was knocked down. She was very lucky, her injuries were horrible but not serious – a broken leg, some very bad cuts and bruising on her left side. I shall never forget the moment I received the call. I was in the middle of a client meeting, an important one. I left them without a thought and drove like a complete maniac to the hospital. When I walked on to the ward, she called out my name and burst into tears. I did not leave her side while she was in hospital. Pete came and went with clean clothes, food and toys. I suddenly took over as the main carer – she was ill and suddenly she needed her Mum, and miraculously that is who I was, a Mum.

I am not saying that all the tension had gone. She still is very different from the little girl I fantasized about but we have an unshakeable bond now, the three of us. She calls us Mum and Dad, quite naturally, and that is who we are, Julie's Mum and Dad.

16

When things go wrong – the breakdown of placements

Matching children with parents cannot and never will be an exact science. You cannot dictate how people feel at any given point in their lives. All social workers can do is look at the files and do their best. It is interesting that some of the most successful matches have been children placed in emergency foster care for a couple of weeks and who have then stayed on for a lifetime. Despite this, a fair number of placements and potential placements do go wrong – most, thankfully, in the introductory period though some much later, when the child has actually been formally adopted. Statistically, the placements made at some distance are the ones most vulnerable, where communication is more difficult, as between social workers and between parents and child.

One of the chief emotions that gets in the way is guilt. Prospective adoptive parents feel guilty if they do not instantly feel what they consider should be the appropriate emotion concerning the child. Many try and force themselves into being and feeling something they are not. Poor communication is also a major contributor, both between partners and also between adoptive parents and social worker. There is a strong feeling that if you reject a child, you may not be offered another one, that you may be branded unsuitable as adoptive parents. It is important to stress that this is not the case. Many prospective adoptive parents, who have felt that for whatever reason they could not proceed with an adoption, have gone on to adopt successfully – particularly if they have reached their decision during the introductory period.

Sadly though, the breakdown of a placement can terminate a couple's attempts at adoption. After all the months of build-up, when the adoption goes wrong the parents are absolutely spent emotionally, exhausted and quite unable to consider going through the whole thing again. It is for this reason, that as well as trying to do the right thing for the child, it is also important to protect yourself and your partner. If things are not going to work, then for heavens sake admit it – sooner, rather than later.

Tom was the youngest of seven siblings – a fairly chaotic family of which already two children were in care. When finally the parents' marriage broke down, Tom went to live with an uncle. However, the level of care there was little better than it had been at home, and finally he was removed and placed with foster parents – a young couple with a new baby of their own.

Tom was eight at the time and from the moment he arrived, he flourished. He stayed with his foster parents for just over a year and when he was nine, a permanent adoptive family was found for him, which coincided with the young foster parents expecting their second child.

Tom moved in with Jim and Jean who were in their early forties. They already had three children by birth – two girls and a boy, and Tom was the youngest by two years. Tom was not a bright child, his deprived background had not helped and it was a real struggle for him to stay in a normal school. Jim and Jean's children, by contrast, were bright and immediately there was pressure on Tom to do better at school. In addition he experienced problems with the structure of his new family's life. Having come from an extremely chaotic household, he'd found life with the young couple and their baby quite acceptable. Being so young, they had had no fixed and entrenched ideas, so far as a routine was concerned, and having so small a baby, things were generally fairly relaxed anyway. Tom had felt perfectly at home. With Jim and Jean, though, things were very different. The family was very close, strict and regimented in the way they behaved. Everyone had to be neat and tidy – beds made, toys put away, church on Sundays... Obviously, there was nothing wrong with any of this but Tom was completely out of his depth. His frustration built and built, until in the end he hit his foster mother and the placement broke down.

Tom was lucky. The young couple who had originally fostered him, when they heard of his plight, asked if they could have him back. Three years later they adopted him.

The young couple were very angry. At the time that he had left them first, they had asked to be allowed to adopt him, but because they were expecting a second baby, they had been refused. They had known they could cope but the social worker was not prepared to listen and as a result, Tom had spent six months of unnecessary suffering, as had the adoptive family with whom he had been wrongly placed.

Social workers are only human – they can only do the best they can, and sometimes they do get it wrong.

> I gave a talk on adoption a few weeks ago and afterwards met one of the audience, called Elizabeth, who told me about her experiences. Having adopted a little girl called Becky, she and her husband had been asked to foster, short-term, a boy called Stewart, who was then eighteen months old. The reason he needed temporary fostering was because his future adoptive parents had needed a rest from him. Elizabeth had been appalled, he had only been with his new prospective adoptive family for three weeks yet already they were asking for respite care. It was not that he was severely disabled or had any particular behaviour disorders, as far as she could see. He was a very frightened, disturbed little boy who needed to be loved. She expressed grave doubts as to the suitability of the adoptive parents and was ignored. Stewart went back and forth between the families like a yo-yo for about six months, and in the end Elizabeth's husband put his foot down. When Stewart came back for yet another 'holiday' (by now far more confused and upset than he had been when they met him) he telephoned the agency and said that Stewart was not going back, he was staying where he was. Eventually everyone saw reason and Stewart, along with Becky, was adopted. When I met Elizabeth, Stewart was nineteen and at university.
>
> Clearly in this case, Elizabeth and her husband could see the obvious problems of the prospective adoptive parents, which they themselves could not admit. Like Tom, Stewart was lucky he had an alternative.

It is perhaps important at this juncture to explain the support team you will have at the time of adoption. The support team will come from two sources. There will be your own social worker, often known as a link worker. She or he will be the one who has prepared the home study and will, if you like, be acting for you. The other support comes from the social worker for the child. Once the adoption order has been made, it is possible that one of the workers will be withdrawn, leaving just one social worker in charge of the case, though of course this depends on the nature of the adoption. It is important, though, to clarify who is in charge of doing what and to make sure you are getting the necessary support. The differences between the two in emphasis terms are these:

- The link worker – in other words your social worker – focuses on the feelings of the adopters and their family. He or she is very much there for them and may well be prepared to intervene on behalf of the adoptive family, if it is felt that the child's social worker is misjudging the situation.

- The social worker for the child is the link for the child with his natural family, if not in a practical way then at least by having the knowledge of what has happened to the child before he came into care. This social worker devotes her energies mainly on the child's behalf, discussing her view on a possible placement and by explaining to the prospective parents the child's point of view on all relevant topics. Her job will be to assist the new parents to understand some of the child's behaviour by linking it to the past, and to advise the new family of any developments in the natural family, which are considered relevant.

As you will see from all this, the support surrounding the introductory period and initial stages, is good, particularly if you are adopting a child from within your own area. In this case, the two social workers will probably know one another and be used to working together which will help, and certainly you will feel that you are not alone. However, once the child is with you and the adoption order has been made, continued support is not always very accessible. Of course in some cases this is the fault of the adopters who feel that they have had enough of social workers and want to distance themselves.

Do not be afraid to ask for help, at any stage. It is not unreasonable to ask for support and you are not putting the adoption at risk by admitting that you are not coping as well as you had hoped – in fact quite the contrary. By the time a child is placed with you, social workers will have invested an enormous amount of time and effort in that placement and they will want it to work quite as much as you do. You do not have to set yourself up as some sort of paragon. Children from the most stable of backgrounds drive their parents to the point of distraction at times, so seek help whenever you need it.

If the placement does look as though it is about to break down, strenuous efforts will be made to try and avoid such an outcome. This could mean bringing in the services of a professional, such as psychotherapy, play-therapy, relief care etc. If these fail and break-down seems unavoidable, even then it does not necessarily mean the end of contact between the adoptive parents and child, if they do still want and need to be in touch.

Normally there will be held what is known as a *disruption meeting*, which brings together all parties concerned, and which will be chaired by an independent person. It is terribly important to recognize that these meetings are not to apportion blame. The social workers involved will be quite as anxious as the parents to try and analyse what went wrong, recognizing that they may have made a mistake in the placement, by underestimating the child's problems, or whatever. Social workers will also be seeking to help parents to understand and deal with their feelings, which are likely to include guilt and humiliation at having apparently 'failed'. This whole concept of adoption breakdown is obviously enormously distressing. All I would say by way of advice is to draw the analogy between how much more sensible it is to break off the engagement before the marriage, than to go ahead with the marriage and end up in the divorce courts.

INTER-COUNTRY ADOPTION

It would be wrong to talk about the break-down of an adoption without quite specifically mentioning inter-country adoption. If you are adopting a child from another country, quite simply it cannot go wrong. Once you have gone through an adoption procedure in the child's country of origin, then the child is yours. He is no longer a citizen of the country in which he was born and even if you may have some months of waiting here in the UK before the adoption is ratified in the British Courts, responsibilities are still clear. The child you are adopting from abroad will have already been rejected once by his own parents. If you are unable to cope with him on your return to the UK, then he will be rejected for the second time and, of course, will end up under the care of the local authority. One of the reasons that local authorities tend to be anti inter-country adoption is that they fear this situation arising. For certainly if things do go wrong, it is their responsibility to sort them out. Small wonder then, that they want to be heavily involved in the run up to such an adoption. I know fairly intimately of one such adoption that has gone wrong. The child is still with temporary foster parents, eighteen months after being taken into care and two years after being brought to this country. Her future is still undecided because her country of origin is demanding her back, the Social Services feel it is inappropriate, the family who brought her out keep changing their mind as to what they want to do, and the foster parents would like to adopt her. Meanwhile poor little Belinda lives a life of uncertainty. It is something, therefore, you should consider very carefully before embarking on inter-country adoption. Inter-country adoption has to be for life, whatever problems you find you have inherited when the child arrives home.

17

Your adopted child and his origins – how to tell a child he is adopted

Many Victorian melodramas have a scene in which the heroine – shortly after the deathbed scene of one of her parents – discovers that she is adopted, with resulting traumas all round. Sadly, such a scenario is not confined to the pages of fiction. Until relatively recently many adopted children were brought up in total ignorance as to their true origins. In some cases they were never to learn the truth. In others, the shock of learning by accident had a profound affect on their lives and, of course, their attitudes to their adoptive parents.

Today there is a much more open attitude to most of life's social dramas and of course adoption is no longer confined to babies who will eventually need to be told. Your adoptive child may have come into your family as a very small child but equally he may be an older child with strong memories of what went before. There are so many possible variations. Your child may come from another country, may be disabled and have a very limited understanding of what adoption means or may have ongoing and continued contact with birth parents or natural siblings. All of these factors influence to a greater or lesser extent, how, when and what you tell your child.

One thing is absolutely certain, though – ADOPTION CANNOT BE KEPT A SECRET. Good relationships can only be built on trust, and trust is dependent upon truth. To deprive your child of the knowledge of his natural origins is to take part in the most serious and damaging of lies.

While we were adopting Michael from Romania, we came in contact with a young, childless couple who were in the process of adopting a newborn baby girl from a maternity home in a village some miles outside Bucharest. The Romanian system of paperwork is really strange and it culminates in the issuing of a Romanian passport, to enable a child to travel to England. On this passport the child's parents are shown as the adoptive parents, since an adoption order has already been granted. The child's birth place is also always stated as the home town of the adoptive parents although, of course, the child was born in Romania. In this particular case the couple concerned had adopted a little girl whose given name was Anna, in other words not a particularly Romanian sounding name. Her passport, therefore, could have been that of their natural child. Our friends said that when they were given the passport, just for one brief moment they suddenly wondered whether they need ever tell Anna that she was adopted. They knew they could never have children by birth, they had looked after Anna since she was two days old, and she already felt like theirs in every respect.

The moment mercifully passed, but it is very understandable that, particularly for childless couples, the desire to make this child you have adopted your own is very strong. The counter-argument for this, though, is equally strong. If you mislead your child and one day he finds out, the chances are he will never forgive you. It is difficult though. Discussing adoption with a child can be rather like talking about sex. If the child does not ask questions, the parents are able to convince themselves that he does not really want to know about his origins. This, of course, is rubbish – all children are curious and *of course* your child will want to know as much detail as possible about his past. Nonetheless, he may well sense that there is a reluctance on your part to discuss details which perhaps you find painful, and so begins a cycle of failed communication which leads to ignorance, misinformation, misguided exploration, pain and fear. Let us look at how best you can deal with the problems which arise in each age group.

THE BABY AND SMALL CHILD

If you are adopting a child who is only just learning to talk or has yet to do so, then it will be your responsibility to tell him that he is adopted. The starting point is to bring the word 'adopted' into the conversation. This should not be at all difficult, because probably at the time you will be going through the adoption process. If the adoption has already happened by the time the child is starting to communicate, then you will be coming round to a meaningful anniversary – the day that we first met you etc., etc. Only you can initiate this conversation. It is, if you like, the first brick in the building. Familiarize the child with the terminology so that he can say confidently, 'I am adopted', even if he does not know precisely what it means. Once this is achieved you need to begin to discuss his origins. If your child comes from overseas, the next step is to identify the child with the country of birth, simply by telling him he was born in Romania or Sri Lanka, or wherever. Whether adoption is from the UK or abroad, the next piece of information he needs to know is that he did not come out of Mummy's tummy but out of another lady's, but that makes him special, because he was chosen by you. From that point onwards questions will start to snowball. You may well find it helpful to start a storybook together illustrated with photographs and drawings, becoming more detailed as your child gets older.

> *In our case we have two sons, only six months apart – Michael from Romania and Charlie, our son by birth. The first book I produced for them was a series of colour photographs showing their home, their playroom, our church, their God-parents, that sort of thing. The only difference between the two books is that on the first page of Michael's book it says, 'I was born in Bucharest, Romania', and there was a picture of University Square in Bucharest, and in Charlie's case, the words say, 'I was born in Oxford', and there was a picture of the John Radcliffe Hospital.*

In other words, you do not have to be too complicated. Small children can only take on board very limited information – they do not want to be saturated with it. In those early days when the boys were only two, it was enough to know that Michael was adopted and that he came from Romania, and Charlie had been born in Oxford. By the age of three, they knew that Charlie had come out of my tummy and that Michael had not. By four, they knew that Michael had come out of someone else's tummy and that someone else was a lady called Lenuta. As I speak they are four-and-a-half and just four respectively, and there have been no questions as yet along the lines of – 'Why didn't I stay with Lenuta? or, why was I adopted? or, why was I brought to England?' We have begun to discuss the orphanage where Michael lived. For example, he has always had an absolute horror of people in white coats. The doctors and nurses in his particular orphanage were very rough and so we have explained that the doctors and nurses in Romania were very busy and therefore were not very kind, because they did not have the time, and that is why he is afraid of white coats. Needless to say, our doctor and dentist disrobe before Michael comes to see them!

I only mention Michael because it is a good way to demonstrate that in fact the information should come in a trickle. He will never be able to tell anyone the moment he learnt he was adopted, because he has always known that he was.

Of course so far we have only tackled the easy bit. As children mature, their questions do become more difficult and sometimes it may be necessary to soften the truth a little, or leave out crucial bits of information until you feel that they are ready to cope with them. Nonetheless, never dodge a question. Being off-hand or avoiding answering, will worry the child and make him feel that there is something wrong.

THE SCHOOL-AGE CHILD

Once your child starts school or even playgroup, or nursery

school, she may be confronted with questions about her origins. Other mothers may well have told the children in your child's class about the fact that she is adopted, and before you know where you are your child will be coming back from school, looking sad and confused and saying things like, 'Why aren't you my real Mummy?' The answer to this is, 'Who gives you cuddles and cooks your meals? Who washes your clothes, who tucks you up in bed and reads you bedtime stories? Who loves you most in all the world?' And the child answers, 'You'. Then you say, 'So, I am your real Mummy, aren't I?' In other words, constantly reassure and stress the links between you.

It is at this stage that the developing of a storybook is particularly valuable, because what you really want to do is arm your child with 'a cover story'. As the child grows older and develops close friendships, she will probably confide in valued peers as to her fears and worries on the subject of her origins. In early school-days though, what you are trying to do is to provide your child with ammunition, to cope with ill-considered and thoughtless enquiries. So build up a reassuring picture as to the stability, strength and ongoing nature of your family unit. Make sure she really understands that despite the fact she is adopted, you are a 'forever and ever family'. Provide her with pictures and drawings, and details of her background. Make her proud of who and what she is, and you should find the book is a great link between you.

As the child grows older – from about the age of eight onwards – she will begin to see her natural parents as real people and begin to make enquiries about them. The one thing you must *never* do is to criticize the natural parents. Do stress that it is not the parents' fault that they could not keep her and this applies even if the parents have done something terribly wrong, like abused her or beaten her. As

I mentioned in an earlier chapter, the old adage 'hate the sin, not the sinner' is the best way to deal with the natural parents' misdemeanours. Think up excuses for them (however hard this is) as to why they behaved as they did, because if you do not provide reasons for their behaviour, then the child will start to blame herself and think it is her fault she was abandoned. As a child approaches adolescence, this is one of the most important danger areas. If the child is not given a really satisfactory reason as to why her parents gave her up, she will start to feel rejected and this sense of rejection will develop into a lack of self-worth that could ruin her whole life.

Of course it is far easier if your child is one of several siblings who were given up for adoption. In our case we have been very lucky in this respect with Michael. His sisters have been adopted by two Italian families – in other words his mother gave up all her children and so there are no grounds for any of them to feel any personal sense of rejection. But of course this is often not the case – in fact sometimes quite the reverse. You may well find yourself in a situation where you have adopted the one child with whom the natural parents could not cope – either because he was the first child who was conceived before they were married, or had a stable relationship, or perhaps the last child which was the one too many, or there again perhaps he was the disabled child, or the most disruptive... In these circumstances, you will have a real battle to try and persuade the child, as he grows, that there is nothing wrong with him – it is the circumstances which are to blame. It is when you are faced with your child's hurt that you may feel it is terribly tempting to start blaming the birth parents, anything to save him feeling that he is in some way responsible, *but please do not do this*. Bear in mind that if you tell your child that his birth parents are bad, then he will assume this means he is bad too.

ADOLESCENCE

Most adolescents go through some form of crisis, as to who they are and what they want out of life. The strong relationship you had with the child may be suddenly in jeopardy, and it is a fact that many young people find it far easier to discuss their worries with somebody other than their parents, adoptive or otherwise. This, of course, particularly applies to the subject of adoption. Adolescents always have such a bad press. They come across as being arrogant, unruly, selfish, loud, noisy, clumsy, and of course they are all of these things, but actually they are also desperately sensitive. They will be only too aware of the pain they may inflict on an adoptive parent by wanting to know more about their origins. This will stop them asking questions and not being able to ask questions will make them angry and resentful towards you, and round and round the resentment will go, making things worse and worse. Of course, you cannot predict the kind of friendships you will have with your child when he is an adolescent, particularly if he is at the stage where you have just tucked him up in his carry cot! Nonetheless, you can lay down some basic relationships which may well help him as the years go by.

In our case we are very lucky, we have a big family and a little family. Our older children are currently thirty-one, twenty-six and eighteen, and we are looking to them for help as our adopted children grow. They are well aware of this and are going to great lengths to form brotherly and sisterly relationships with their young siblings, which they are the first to say is no problem at all since they love them to bits! You could consider this sort of relationship for your own child. You may not have older children of your own, but you could think very carefully about God-parents and perhaps select at least one God-parent who is some years younger than you and your partner, and therefore is more likely to be in tune with your child's problems, as he comes to adulthood himself.

As with any adolescent, the advice has to be to keep communicating. It is not easy, it requires a great deal of stamina but while you are still talking to one another, you stand a good chance of helping them to come to terms with whatever their problems may be.

ADOPTING AN OLDER CHILD

If you are adopting an older child, who is only too aware of his background problems, you may feel that this chapter on telling is not for you. This is not the case because your child is likely to have very many unanswered questions. It is a fact that people desperately under-rate children and their ability to understand. Even really good social workers tend to be a little scanty on the explanations as to what is happening next, due, usually, to pressure of work and lack of time. Much of what may have happened to your child in his life may be a mystery to him. Once he feels safe within your home, he may try to blot it out and this could be very damaging, because at some stage all that hurt and anger has to come out. Here again, this is where a life storybook is of much value. Mercifully, today, most children come with a fairly extensive, detailed dossier on what has happened to them so far. Nonetheless, it is likely that not all the details will be there, and you would be well advised to ask your social worker to fill in any obvious gaps. The more information you have, the better. Once your child is settled in your home, probably the very best way to break the ice on his past is to start building up one of these books. If he is very reluctant to even do this, start with a scrapbook about the present and you may then be able to work backwards, once he has got the idea as to what you are doing.

I was talking to an adoptive mother the other day, who told me that in the course of her son preparing his life storybook, he wrote these words at the end of a particular section: 'I always thought it was my fault, that these things kept happening to me, and now I know it isn't.' A wonderful confirmation that this sort of exercise is so very worthwhile.

INTER-COUNTRY ADOPTION

So far as tracing birth parents when inter-country adoption has taken place, everything will depend on the quality of the paperwork you acquired at the time of your child's adoption. Some people, particularly adopting from South America, have no idea as to the child's birth parents. This may not be their fault – often the child was simply abandoned on an orphanage or hospital steps, in which case there may be very little that can be done. All I would stress, however, is that along with all the other pressures associated with adopting a child from abroad, do try and find out as much information as you can AT THE TIME OF THE ADOPTION IN THE CHILD'S COUNTRY OF ORIGIN. If the child you are adopting is a baby, particularly a new baby, the trail will not have yet gone cold. It may well be possible to locate the parents, to even meet them. If years later you try to unravel your child's past, it will be hopeless. In most of the countries in which adoptions take place, there are so many unwanted babies it will be almost impossible to distinguish yours from anyone else's. I know it is difficult, you will be fighting so many emotions at the same time, but adoption is forever and you have to look – not just to the moment – but to how your child will feel in twenty years time when you can offer him nothing of his past.

If your child comes from another country, consider the following to help him keep in touch with his origins:

- Learning the language, as a family.

- Make sure there are maps and posters of the child's country of birth in the home.

- Learn to cook food from the child's country of origin and if there is such a thing, visit restaurants serving dishes of the same.

- Try and find other adoptive children from the same country.

- Ask travel agencies for brochures and details of the country, to make up a scrapbook.

- Buy some tapes of the country's national music.

- If you can afford it, travel to the child's country of origin.

Above all, give your child a sense of pride in his country of birth. If that country is desperately deprived, even if that country has a very bad press, look for the positive aspects and build on these.

Your child may also be a different colour to yourself – in most instances parents will be white and their adoptive children black. Clearly the differences between you cannot be ignored. Even today, with great emphasis being placed on trying to stamp out racial discrimination, it exists, and even the word 'black' has unfortunate connotations. Think of how often we use the word in a derogatory way – a black mood, a black mark, blackmail, blackmarkets, etc., etc. It is difficult to give black a positive image. We have all read stories of black children trying to scrub themselves white, which is such an appalling concept, and the situation is more likely to occur where the black child is in a white family. Here again what you must do is to build up in the child a sense of pride in being black.

Perhaps the best advice of all is constantly to try and put yourself in your child's position. You have probably grown up knowing precisely who your mother and father were. Try and imagine what it would be like if you did not, or if they had rejected you, or beaten you, or abused you. Putting yourself in your child's position is the most helpful thing you can do, that, and building up a security blanket around the child. From a very early age, Michael's favourite word has been 'safe'. I used it when he had a very limited vocabulary and when he had appalling nightmares. I would tell him again and again that he was safe. Even now, in often very inappropriate moments like when he has cut his knee or had a row with his brother, he still needs to be told he is 'safe'. You cannot tell your child too often that you love him, you cannot give him enough hugs and reassurance. Couple this with being honest and sensitive in all your discussions on his past and you will be well on the way to a well-balanced, happy child.

THE BIRTH FAMILY

In discussing the question of telling, we have assumed that the child has become separated from his origins. Increasingly today, agencies are moving towards keeping children in touch, certainly with their siblings and quite often with their birth parents, or grandparents. This is a two-edged sword. Such an arrangement can be deeply distressing and difficult for adoptive parents, since they feel that the child is not really theirs. From a child's point of view it also can be very upsetting, for it may build up a sense of ongoing insecurity. Nonetheless, particularly if you are adopting or fostering an older child, keeping some form of communication going with the birth family may be in the best interests of the child, since he simply may not want to sever connections with his family. Very often, once the child is settled in a permanent placement, the communications between him and his birth family do dwindle and in some instances this may well be a good thing. However, when the child does have a strong and ongoing need to be in touch with his birth family, this is something you simply have to respect, and if you are not prepared to facilitate this then you must not go ahead with adopting the child. All you can do is to hope that the good sense of all concerned will ultimately prevail if things become tricky. Certainly you may well find that some children faced with visits from birth parents, become very distressed at the prospect. If they are deeply distressed before they go and even more distressed when they come back, then maybe your social worker would be prepared to apply to the court to have access terminated, or at any rate greatly reduced. It is a question really of going with the flow, seeing how your child develops once he has settled in his new home, as to what part this birth family will play in his future life. One thing is for certain though, you must not try and drive a wedge between a child and his birth family. If you do you will regret it, for he will resent it in the years ahead.

18

Tracing

Anyone who adopts a child now (or has done so in the last ten to fifteen years), will have been given considerably more information about the child than in previous decades. With the child comes a copy of 'Form E', which is basically a fairly comprehensive record of everything that is known about the child and his past including, of course, details of his parents and birth family. In the past, adoption records contained very scant information, particularly so far as the father was concerned, and indeed the circumstances of the adoption. At the time it was not recognized that it was important for adopted people to have information on their background, and whole generations grew up with no hope of ever acquiring any knowledge about their birth families.

This openness about adoption today is the result of a number of circumstances coming together:

- More children being adopted now have their own memories of their early life and birth parents, which form a base from which questioning can begin.

- Since 1975 adopted children, once they reach the age of

eighteen, have access to their birth certificates and therefore information about at least one of their parents. Adoptive parents are well aware of this which encourages them to provide the information which they know their children can find out anyway.

- In May 1991, the General Register Office in Stockport began operating an Adoption Contact Register. For the first time, this enables birth relatives to register their desire to be put in touch with an adopted person. If you are seeking an adopted child, or if you are an adopted child yourself, the Contact Register is of equal benefit. By submitting an application form and paying a relatively small fee, not only can you register your wish for contact but you can also see whether anyone has sought contact with you.

- This is only guesswork but I suspect that adopted children no longer stand out in a crowd, because, sadly, of the massive increase in broken homes. So many children now no longer live with both people who created them. Many children are born outside marriage, many share their homes with half-siblings or siblings who are in fact no relation at all. All this is not very far removed from adoption. While one would much prefer to see a greater number of solid marriages in which children grow up in security, the one positive spin-off of today's chaotic society must be to make adopted children feel less odd!

At some stage in your adopted child's life, he is probably going to want to trace his natural parents. This may not be as one might assume, as a teenager when, frankly, life is confusing enough without adding to it. It may be triggered off in later life either when you, the adoptive parents die, or when your adopted child becomes a parent herself. I have a friend who is adopted, and the trigger for her was the moment she gave birth to her first child. She could not believe the intensity of love she felt for this baby, and could not come to terms with the fact that her mother had given her up. She had to know why.

Sometimes adopted 'children' seek birth parents when things have gone terribly wrong with their own lives – when their marriage has broken up, when they have somehow lost their way, or they have fallen out with their adoptive parents. Clearly it is your duty as an adoptive parent to help your child in every way to trace her birth parents. To deny her this is to deny her a vital part of herself and it will rebound on you. If from the very beginning you demonstrate true and genuine support, then your child will not feel the need to be secretive and will tell you how the search is going, and seek your advice. This in turn will enable you to give your child much needed support, when at times she feels despondent or frightened about what she is doing. One of the very best pieces of advice you can give her is not to tackle tracing like a bull at a gate and instead to use intermediaries, both to protect her feelings and that of her natural parents. Secondly, make sure that she has access to some form of counselling – and not just yours, *professional* counselling which most agencies will be only too happy to provide. Children do need to look at why they want to trace their birth parents and also to prepare themselves for what may be a considerable shock. Inevitably, children build up images of how they imagine their birth parents look, behave and feel about them. Of course the reunion between the child and natural parent can be a wonderful thing which works well and enhances everyone's life, but equally it can be a disaster and a series of terrible emotional shocks. For your part, you can pave the way by making sure that your child has no illusions about her birth parents. This does not mean you should be critical. As discussed in the previous chapter, this is quite wrong but you should, nonetheless, pull no punches and make sure that your child has a good, solid, truthful basis of understanding about the circumstances of her adoption, and the likely attitude of her natural parents to her.

Let us look at the tracing procedure step-by-step, and here I am quite specifically talking about UK adoption:

1. Obviously the starting point is to contact the agency through whom the adoption took place. It may be that you have to go no further than this. The agency may have kept in touch with the birth parents and after the child has received counselling, would be very prepared to act as an intermediary between your child and the birth parents, to see whether the parents would like contact with their child.

2. If the agency are unable to help you to trace the parents, then it would be worth getting in touch with the Contact Register in case either parent has expressed a desire to meet the child. If not, there are various organizations who are helpful in tracing. These are listed at the back of this book, but the most well known is probably NORCAP.

3. Having found out as much information as you can, it may mean that you will end up with an exhaustive random search through birth and marriage registers at St. Catharine's House, for up-to-date information on the birth parents. Their marriage certificates would provide addresses for example.

4. Assuming one or either of the birth parents are eventually located, then it is as well to ask a social worker or counsellor to act as an intermediary. Start with letters which might then build up to telephone calls, and ultimately a meeting. Do try and dissuade your child from rushing in. It could well prove a terrible shock to the birth parents who may not have told their new families anything about the fact that they had a child who they gave away.

Here are three case histories with very different outcomes:

Simon
Simon was conceived when his mother, Sally, was at teacher training college. Sally would not disclose the name of the father and was very ambivalent about adoption, but went ahead because really she had no choice. Records show that she remained in contact with the agency for some time after the adoption order was made, clearly seeking reassurance about her decision and regularly asking for news about Simon. Simon was placed as the second adopted child with a childless couple, who enjoyed a very traditional, middle-class lifestyle and had a very commonsense attitude to adoption and adoptive children. They made sure their children were aware of their status in an appropriate way, and invited them to seek whatever contact they felt was necessary with their birth parents, with their full support.

In late adolescence, Simon embarked on an accountancy training course but subsequently abandoned this and took 'A' levels in media studies instead. He went to college on the south coast to do a degree course. At about this time, his adoptive parents moved from the house they had lived in ever since Simon's adoption. Being a responsible woman, Simon's adoptive mother wrote to the adoption agency to advise them of the move, in case Simon's birth mother ever wanted to make contact. At the same time, she sent news of Simon's progress.

Sally had indeed been diligent in maintaining contact with the agency over the years. She had spent long periods of her life abroad, but when she was out of the country she had gone to the trouble of nominating a contact person, to keep in touch with the agency concerning Simon's progress. Within three weeks of Simon's adoptive mother writing to the agency, Sally had replied with a long letter. She had never married but had twin daughters aged three. After having travelled abroad extensively, she had now settled in the UK and was living on the south coast, only fifteen miles from the town where Simon was at college. Clearly, Simon had never been far from her thoughts. She was very sensitive to the feelings of the adoptive parents but, nonetheless, remained deeply emotional about Simon.

The adoption agency left Simon's adoptive parents to decide whether or not to talk to Simon. For them there was no question of doing anything else. Initially Simon's inclination was to wait until he felt he was ready to make contact with Sally. He did not want the initiative taken from him. However, within a matter of weeks, he did make contact with the agency direct and had many discussions with them about whether or not he should proceed to make contact with Sally. In fact, as part of his media studies, Simon had made a video on adoption and this had helped him to address many of the issues he now faced.

Eventually Simon began to exchange letters with Sally, the agency acting as intermediary. This prompted a very emotional response from Sally and the agency received many anguished calls from her, asking whether Simon had expressed any desire for them to meet.

Simon saw his records and appeared, on the surface, to be very cautious and measured about the idea of meeting Sally. Then, quite suddenly, it seemed as if he could no longer contain himself. He telephoned Sally and within half an hour they had met. They spent the weekend together, taking time to get to know one another and discovered many common interests. They tried to help each other with their feelings – Sally to come to terms with her guilt, Simon to come to terms with his anger. After several weeks of meeting frequently, Sally and the adoptive parents met, and got along extremely well.

The adoptive parents in this particular case had managed to remain supportive in Simon's search, because they were confident about Simon's affection for them. They were very aware of the importance of Simon being able to meet his birth mother and Sally, too, was very sensitive to the feelings of the adoptive parents. The whole thing worked because of considerable generosity on the part of everyone, and Sally and Simon's life is richer as a result.

Victoria
Victoria was conceived when her mother, Jennie, was fifteen. Jennie was the daughter of an aspiring middle-class couple. She has been educated at private school but had taken up with what her parents considered to be a very unsuitable young man. Victoria's father was called Eddie, a working-class boy with a background of

stealing, and at the time of meeting Jennie, he was on probation.

Jennie's parents were horrified by the association between their daughter and this boy who was considerably older than her at twenty. He was also wild, had a police record and, quite clearly, came from 'the wrong side of town'. The parents believed that they could end the friendship and forbade the young couple to meet. The father was very diligent – dropping off Jennie outside the cinema and collecting her at the end of the evening. Of course Jennie wasn't going to the cinema, she was visiting Eddie, and pregnancy was the result.

When Jennie's pregnancy was discovered, she was sent to her grandparents for the confinement, and it was concealed from friends and the rest of the family. Eddie was sent to approved school for unlawful sexual intercourse, from which he absconded several times to see Jennie. However, as Jennie's pregnancy developed, the relationship waned. When the baby was born, she was placed with foster parents and then with adoptive parents. Eddie saw the baby once but made no objection to her being adopted.

Victoria had an unspectacular childhood, with apparently no problems relating to her adoptive status. She married relatively young and had three children, but then her marriage went through a difficult patch and her husband threatened to seek custody of the children. It was at this point of crisis that Victoria sought information about her birth parents. In spite of misgivings on the part of the social worker undertaking the counselling, information was passed on. Undoubtedly Victoria was demonstrating a degree of instability and had become completely obsessive about knowing of her past.

Almost immediately Victoria located Eddie, as his

mother had not moved from the address on the birth records. Once father and daughter met, they decided to locate Jennie. Eddie had married but was divorced and had no other children. Jennie had married and had a daughter. She was living in circumstances with which her parents must have been pleased – a classic middle-class lifestyle.

Eddie had retained much anger towards Jennie and her parents, feeling that their rejection of him had caused much of his problems in life. He and Victoria approached Jennie, in a fairly aggressive and insensitive manner, and she made it clear that she wanted nothing to do with either of them. Maybe it would have been different if Victoria had approached her birth mother alone, but as obviously Victoria and Eddie had formed such a strong alliance, Jennie probably felt that there was no need for her to be involved.

What followed then was nothing short of intimidation by Victoria and Eddie – harrassing phone calls at Jennie's work place, late night visits ... Victoria finally left her husband and children and moved in with Eddie. They presented themselves very much as a couple and left those professionals with whom they had contact, in no doubt that their relationship had a sexual element. Research shows that there can be a sexual attraction between birth parents and their children, particularly when they have not lived as father and daughter, as in this case. Eddie and Victoria also harrassed the agency concerned, indeed were very aggressive to anybody connected with the adoption, and so alienated themselves from their families, which probably reinforced the strength of their own alliance.

Clearly, Victoria was an awkward person. It was very

unfortunate that she made contact with her father first, rather than her mother. Things might have been very different had it been the other way round.

David
David was conceived when his parents, Jack and Liz, were nineteen and eighteen respectively. Both of them were living with their own families and were in no position to support a baby. Together they decided it was best for everybody that their child should be placed for adoption. They were a bright, committed couple with a strong bond. David was placed as a second adoptive child, with a relatively affluent family, who were in middle age.

Jack and Liz remained together, although they never married. After some years they had a daughter. It was Liz who became preoccupied with finding David, particularly as his eighteenth birthday approached. As a result, Jack and Liz contacted the agency who had placed him, in the hopes that they would make contact with the adoptive parents. The agency declined to help, because they were prohibited legally from contacting the adoptive parents. However, with persistence and some luck, Jack and Liz were able to discover David's adoptive name, and from there were able to trace his adoptive parents. Without acting through an intermediary, they approached the adoptive parents direct, and were rebuffed quite aggressively by the father, who said he would not be prepared to tell David of their contact. With persistence, though, ultimately David's adoptive mother told him of the contact and David was fairly speedily in touch. Initially he was a little hesitant with his birth parents, but soon he was spending protracted periods of time with them and thus virtually rejected his adoptive parents. It is easy to see why. David was in the middle of impressionable adolescence. Jack and Liz were still relatively young, unconventional in lifestyle, left wing, their appearances trendy and off-beat – in other words, in all respects different, and to David more attractive than his adoptive parents, who were affluent, conservative, reserved and relatively old.

The result was confusion for everyone – confusion, above all, for David, who felt a tremendous sense of divided loyalties; jealousy, anger and hurt on the part of the adoptive parents; and since Jack and Liz were genuinely nice people, a sense of guilt and concern about the hornets' nest they had created for their son and his adoptive parents.

It is very easy to sit in judgement on such a case. Perhaps David's adoptive parents should have been more supportive to his contacting his birth parents. Clearly, he had to make the contact almost in spite of them which in turn forced him into an either/or situation. Instead of reacting aggressively against Jack and Liz's contact, they should have offered their cooperation but suggested to David that he slowed down the contact process, beginning initially with letters. It is a fact that adoptive parents are often considerably older than birth parents and perhaps this should be a lesson to us all. Perhaps they were too busy pursuing their middle-age aspirations, rather than providing a stimulating home base for their adoptive son.

So you can see, like everything else concerning adoption, tracing can be a minefield. So much depends on the attitude of the child. I have a friend who is in his late forties, who is adopted, and has absolutely no wish to trace his birth parents. He was brought up on a glorious country estate in the middle of the Lake District, by two people who loved him dearly and gave him the most wonderful life. He has no desire, as he puts it, to know the seamy aspects of his conception – he is just jolly grateful he ended up where he did! I am not saying this attitude is right but perhaps it does help to put adoption in perspective. Being adopted is just one aspect of a child's life. It is not the core and while it is important, it is not *the* most important thing. Be open and truthful with your child on all aspects of adoption but keep it in perspective.

SECTION 4

Fostering

19

Why foster?

So why foster a child? Surely adoption is so much more satisfactory, after all the child is yours forever. How do you cope with learning to love a child and then watch it go? What sort of people foster and how can they?

Most foster parents have children of their own, either by birth or adoption, or a mix of the two. Usually they start when their children are still quite young, and usually they are people who are fairly involved with the community as a whole – with scouts or guides, the church, or the local school. Indeed the best foster family embraces the wider community – it is not a tight family unit. A tight family unit might sound like a good thing to be and so it is, but a family which runs very much an open house is better material for fostering. Too close and intimate a unit will be difficult for a visiting child to penetrate. The age of the parents is not nearly so relevant as with adopted children. There is a minimum age of twenty-one but no maximum age, although obviously common sense prevails. Some parents foster on a long-term basis, others offer short-term fostering and emergency care. Some foster parents specialize in particular types of children, who have a specific medical condition.

So why foster? The best reason is because there is a considerable shortage of good foster carers, particularly those who are prepared to offer short-term foster care. While it is now recognized that children's homes are no place for most children in care, whether temporarily or permanently, it is also equally recognized that being a foster parent is not an easy job. One parent, usually the woman, will essentially need to look on her job as foster parent as a full-time one, which means that the family will have to survive on one income. Although some foster parents' allowances are generous, in some areas they are extremely meagre and certainly there is very little element of reward. If you are lucky, the allowance you receive will just about cover the costs of fostering the child, but there will certainly be nothing left over for life's little luxuries. When you add to this the fact that you will be often taking into your home extremely distressed children whose behaviour will be appalling and who will upset you and your family, it is hard to see why anybody fosters at all. Yet if you love children, it is the most marvellously rewarding thing to do. I have talked to a number of foster parents in the preparation of this book and some of the stories they have to tell are amazing. Many have kept in touch with their foster children over the years, many have had them back again and again as social workers struggle to rehabilitate them with their parents. Sometimes they have taken a child in on an emergency basis for a few days and he is still there – fifteen years later. The warmth and generosity of good foster parents knows no bounds. It must be wonderful to see a terrified, bewildered child, blossoming under your care, not once but again and again, over the years.

I mentioned the typical foster parent. You may well be asking what sort of qualifications you need. While I said that most foster parents are a couple, single people are considered though it is not usual. A single person cannot live on the foster care allowance so unless you have private means, it would be very difficult to survive financially and foster children. However, single people do become involved in respite care, as do childless couples. It may be that your job throws you into a situation where it would be easy to become involved with fostering – for example if you are a nursery nurse and from time to time children need fostering for the weekend. In other words, there is no actual barrier to fostering as a single person, it is just not so easy to organize.

Similarly with childless couples, there is no barrier against being foster parents. It is just that childless couples on the whole are not so attracted to the concept and, of course, do not have the same degree of experience with children as a couple who already have some of their own. I suppose childless couples are far more likely to look to adoption. If they do not want to adopt, it is probably because they do not want children at all.

As a foster parent you do have to be a fairly forthright person. You will have a link worker who, if you like, will represent you and your interests. Nonetheless, you will be directly involved in planning meetings, case conferences and court appearances. As the foster parent, increasingly it is being recognized that you probably know the child better than anyone, and your advice as to how the child's future should be handled is starting to be really valued. You have to have the confidence to liaise with a range of professional people – doctors, psychiatrists, judges, lawyers, and it is important that, without being arrogant, you are able to express your views in order to do the very best for the child in your care. What I am really saying is that it is no good being a foster parent and a shrinking violet. As well as being able to express yourself, forcibly if necessary, you also have to enjoy meeting people and being involved in group discussions. If you are a very private person who likes to keep yourself to yourself, you will not be a good foster parent.

I think for most of us, if we try and conjure up how we see a foster mother, we see a rather large, cuddly, jolly, smiling, noisy woman in her middle years, with a big lap and a big heart to match, who everyone adores but who, nonetheless, has rules which must be obeyed. It has to be said that there are many variations on this theme!

In trying to analyse whether you feel you would make good foster parents, you need to consider very carefully the children you may already have in your family. Quite recently the Social Services in my area did some research on foster carers' children, to try and gain views as to how they felt about their parents' activities. Quite a number of them said that they wished that their parents did not foster. Having said that, it is interesting that a fair proportion of foster carers' children go on to foster themselves, so this obviously cuts both ways. A number of the children said they wished that they were consulted more. Social workers come and go and might, or might not, acknowledge their existence but never involve them in the decision to take in a child, or indeed ask their advice or views on how the child is doing, or should be handled. In other words, they want more status. Many expressed dissatisfaction with the practical aspects. Saturdays, they said, were usually ruined because it is the day the foster children's natural parents visit. This means that they cannot go out, that the house has to be cleaned up, that the foster children become tense and tearful and everyone is on edge. Certainly it is not the fun day that Saturday is supposed to be. They also said they found it quite difficult when foster children attended the same school as they did, which, of course, often happens.

Usually the foster child would want to tag along, even be very clingy and tearful and this could prove extremely embarrassing, particularly if the foster child's behaviour was in any way out of order.

These then were the children's main grouses and they are very realistic and understandable ones. Certainly your own children will not be able to do the same things with you that they would be able to do if you did not take in foster children. There will not be so much money to go round for holidays and days out. As indicated, Saturdays will often be a write-off and foster children, by definition, will take up a disproportionate amount of parental time, so that the foster carers' own children may well have to fend for themselves, more than they would like. There will also be the danger of an element of uncertainty and insecurity, because if you are a short term foster carer, you never know who will be landing on your doorstep next. Of course foster parents can, and frequently do, ask for a break now and again, so that they can go on holiday with their own children or simply give their children one hundred per cent attention while they are going through GCSEs, or whatever, but this does not always work out. Good foster parents develop such a sense of responsibility that when it comes to the crunch, they will not be able to refuse anyone who really needs a home – even if it is not in their own children's best interests to do so.

Against this, of course, your children will grow up with a very realistic understanding of the world and how it works. With luck they will learn to be generous-spirited, to share and to give, to offer comfort. They will become sociable creatures, used to being able to mix with a wide variety of people. They will not be shy children. So much depends on your own abilities to keep tension at a minimum and fun at a maximum. Can you genuinely run a lovely, happy, open house, where children come and go, and while they are with you feel as secure as is possible in their difficult lives? Can you give your own children special time, no matter what the problems, and a sense of deep-down security? If so, then the benefits will outweigh the disadvantages so far as your children are concerned. Once again, communication is the vital ingredient. If night after night you are sitting up with little Johnny because he has just been removed from his step-father's house where he was being raped every night, then you are going to be tired and scratchy with your own children. They will understand that little Johnny has been through some terrible experiences but there will still be an understandable element in their thinking which says little Johnny's problems are not theirs – he is making our mother cross and scratchy and that is not fair. The only way round this is to be super-human and I suppose that is the last and most vital ingredient for a foster parent!

20

How to become a foster parent

About 36,000 children a year are fostered in England and Wales and the fact is there are not enough foster homes to go round. For this reason, if you are seriously interested in becoming a foster parent your local authority is likely to be very enthusiastic, assuming they deem you to be suitable. There are three categories of fostering:

- Short-term/temporary fostering.

- Long-term/permanent fostering.

- Private fostering.

By far the most needed category is for short-term fostering. Most of this book has been dedicated to adoption and by inference, therefore, the children we have been discussing have, for the most part, suffered some major loss or abuse, or at best, insecurities in their lives. By definition, if they are needing a new family other than their birth family, there must be some very big drama to have made this necessary. This is not always the case with fostering. Sometimes children need temporary foster care because their mother is ill, or their father has lost his job or their home has been repossessed. These, of course, are serious problems but they do not involve the maltreatment of the child, nor is the child necessarily very disturbed or difficult as a result. I am not trying to paint a rosy picture of fostering, but the fact is that statistically, most of the children who come into foster care ultimately end up being returned to one or both parents.

Fostering can be undertaken by various means:

- Being a short-term foster carer does not mean that as a general rule you will be rung at three o'clock in the morning by your link worker, asking if you could take in eighteen-month-old triplets by breakfast time. But it could happen! Children usually need to be removed from their families in a hurry because something has happened, and very often it is fairly dramatic because the children are at risk. You are likely to receive a frightened, bewildered, angry little person who is going to need a lot of reassurance.

- Long-term or permanent foster care is not such a crying need, although, do not misunderstand me – long-term foster parents are needed. You might ask why a child would be fostered in the long term, rather than adopted. The usual reason is that the child still has a close bond with one or both parents and does not want to belong to another family, although it may be inappropriate for the child to ever live with his family again. Long-term fostering does not offer the same legal security as adoption and usually terminates when the child reaches eighteen. Occasionally, long-term fostering leads to adoption but essentially fostering and adoption should be looked at as two completely different issues.

- Private fostering. Sometimes parents make arrangements directly with friends to privately foster their child or children. The legal definition of a private foster is when a child under sixteen is looked after for more than twenty-eight days, by someone who is neither a relation nor a guardian. It makes no difference whether a payment is made or not – it is still private fostering.

  Local authorities are not very keen on private fostering. It is the local authority's duty to be satisfied about the welfare of all foster children in the area, including those in private fostering arrangements, but no payment or foster care allowance is made to private foster parents. Any financial arrangements will be made by the parents. It is required that the local authority Social Services Department is notified in advance, of any proposal to foster a child privately between six and thirteen weeks before the fostering starts. Of course in practice such notice may not be possible. As with any kind of fostering, private fostering is likely to be necessary because of an unplanned incident, such as an accident or illness. Nonetheless, when a private fostering arrangement commences, the local authority must be advised and they will want to come and see the child and the foster home, and are likely to continue to monitor progress every six weeks or so. It should perhaps be stated that the local authority do have the power to forbid fostering or impose conditions where children are being fostered by private arrangement.

The procedure for applying to be a foster parent is basically the same as for adoption. You should contact your local authority who will send a social worker to see you and arrange to undertake a home study, assuming they consider you to be suitable. During the process of your home study, you will be expected to attend foster care meetings. When a couple are applying to adopt, although the local authority like them to attend meetings, it is not compulsory. However, so far as foster carers are concerned, most local authorities feel that it is essential that they become involved with the whole foster care structure in the area, by attending meetings and meeting other foster carers. Being foster parents, as we have already discussed, is very much a team effort. While it is accepted that some adoptive parents do not want to become involved in meetings and seminars, foster carers really need to steep themselves in the whole business. Having said that, the home study process is probably not quite as arduous as for an adoptive parent and as mentioned in Chapter Nineteen, the rules concerning age are less stringent.

You will be approved for fostering one, two or three children in a specific age range, though that age range is fairly broad – it is likely to be, say 'under thirteen', or whatever, unless you are very specific yourself. Once your home study is completed, as with adoption, it goes through the panel for approval, but unlike adoption, it is reviewed annually. In other words, the panel look at foster carers in their area each year. Once you have been approved as a foster carer, you may well find you are thrown in at the deep end fairly quickly, according to the needs of your community. As with age, racial differences are not so strict – if you are a white family, you will not be precluded from fostering black or mixed-race children, it is simply a question of meeting the needs as they arise.

What is essential is that you build up trust and understanding with your link worker for she is, in theory, on your side to ensure that you get what support you need.

FOSTER CARE ALLOWANCE

As mentioned in Chapter Nineteen, you are not going to get rich by being a foster parent and there is an enormous regional variation as to what you are likely to be paid. Quoting from the BAAF booklet on foster care, they say that in April 1992 the allowance paid per child ranged from £28.07 to £148.72 a week for children under five and from £58.24 and £239.44 per week for a young person aged seventeen. Extra allowances are available for children who have special needs. For example, a child with a physical or mental disability needing round the clock care and many visits to hospital, will attract a higher allowance. There are certain categories of foster parents who are sometimes called *specialist foster carers*. They may have required some special training to cope with a quite specific category of disabled child, and this again will attract higher allowances.

Being away from home, in a strange house, with strange people, as a small child is not easy. Bearing in mind that this move may well have been precipitated by some family crisis, it is difficult to immediately see the positive side of foster care from the child's point of view. Obviously being fostered in a family is an enormous advance on being placed in an institution. To be absorbed into somebody else's family may be confusing, to receive the love and comfort offered by family life, albeit not your own, is a very positive thing. Sometimes children can remain in the same school and therefore retain their friends, which is a huge help. Even if they have to move some distance away and have to literally start their lives again, there can still be many happy aspects to being a foster child – learning how other people live, learning to share, these are all valuable lessons for life.

Ideally, when your foster child arrives, there should be some accompanying information concerning the child's routine, what he or she likes to eat, favourite toys, books, this sort of thing. In practice this does not always happen, particularly in an emergency, in which case you are simply going to have to take your lead from the child. Obviously you should be made aware of the religious or ethnic group to which the child belongs, as this could affect the child's diet. In other words, your aim is to quite literally provide a home from home.

Conclusion

In a good year about seven thousand children are adopted from within the UK. Except for the bumper period caused by the revolution in Romania, only a handful are adopted from abroad. Better than nothing – yes, of course it is. Yet set against the desperate need of millions of children worldwide, it is not much of an effort for a population of over fifty million people.

In this book I have tried to show adoption and fostering, warts and all. Adoption is not easy and, of course, it should not be. Nonetheless, there are ways in which the whole procedure could be made so much more workable and be of huge benefit to children and parents alike.

It seems to me that adoption does not receive the status it deserves. Social workers attached to the various adoption agencies often seem inefficient and ponderous in their decisions. Much of this is due to a chronic shortage of staff and underfunding. It is costing the State huge sums of money to keep children in care when what, of course, they need is a family. If more staff and funding were deployed they would more than pay for themselves, and far more important, more children would be given a chance of a happy and stable life. Adoption should be seen as a positive thing, as a celebration, and yet it seems to have such a negative image. Adoptive parents are not seen as *real* parents, and this attitude crops up in a number of ways – for example, in the fact that there is no maternity allowance for adoptive mothers. Let's face it, adoption is not on anyone's list of priorities, and yet it should be. Unhappy, mistreated children of today become tomorrow's misfits and criminals – a bitter legacy of our inability to give appropriate love, security and care when it is needed.

Adoption should be given a better press. Couples with children of their own should be encouraged to consider adoption as an alternative to creating more. People finding it difficult to have children should be encouraged to see adoption not as a last resort but more as a wonderful opportunity to help someone. In conclusion I can only say that for both my husband and I, nothing in our lives has been so worthwhile and fulfilling as adopting Michael. Giving one child a chance may not seem much of a way to save the world, but it is going to mean everything to that child. A happy, secure, loving family is every child's right – perhaps you can provide this for someone because EVERY CHILD COUNTS.

DEBORAH FOWLER
OXFORD
1993

Useful addresses

GENERAL INFORMATION

British Agency for Adoption and Fostering (BAAF)
11 Southwark Street
London SE1 1RQ
Tel: 071 407 8800

40 Shandwick Place
Edinburgh
EH2 4RT
Tel: 031 225 9285 (for Scotland)
Contact the London Office for details of you nearest BAAF centre.

Parent to Parent Information on Adoption Services (PPIAS)
Lower Boddington
Daventry
Northants NN11 6YB
Tel: 0327 60295

National Organisation for the Counselling of Adoptees
  and their Parents, (NORCAP)
3 New High Street
Headington
Oxford OX3 5SJ
Tel: 0865 750554

The Catholic Children's Society
49 Russell Hill Road
Purley
Surrey CR8 2XB
Tel: 081 668 2181

The National Association for the Childless
318 Summer Lane
Birmingham B19 3RC
Tel: 021 359 4887

Parents for Children
222 Camden High Street
London NW1 8QR
Tel: 081 485 7526

INTER-COUNTRY ADOPTION

STORK
Dan y Graig
Balaclava Road
Glals
Swansea SA7 9HJ
Tel: 0306 880189

Overseas Adoption Helpline 071-226 7666

USEFUL ADDRESSES

Home Office, Immigration and Nationality Dept.
Lunar House
Wellesley Road
Croydon, Surrey CR9 2BY (ask for leaflet ROW 117)
Tel: 081 686 0688

Migrant Trust
8 Musters Road
West Bridgeford
Nottingham NG2 7AQ
Tel: 021 359 4887

Adopted Romanian Children's Society (ARC)
150 Montague Mansions
London W1H 1LA

POST ADOPTION SERVICES

Post Adoption Centre
8 Torriano Mews
Torriano Avenue
London NW5 2RZ

NORCAP – See address under General Information

PPIAS – See address under General Information

Adoption Counselling Centre
Family Care
21 Castle Street
Edinburgh EH2 3DN

After Adoption
2nd Floor
Lloyds House
22 Lloyd Street
Manchester M2 5WA

Natural Parents' Support Group
10 Alandale Crescent
Garforth
Leeds LS25 LDH

TRACING BIRTH PARENTS

For birth certificates apply to:

The Registrar General
Adopted Children's Register
Titchfield
Fareham, Hants PO15 5RV
   (for England and Wales)

The General Registrar's Office
New Register House
Edinburgh EH1 3YI (for Scotland)

Adoption Contact Register
Smedley Hydro
Trafalgar Road
Birkdale
Southport, Merseyside PR8 2HH
   (for England and Wales)

Adoption Contact Register
Family Care
21 Castle Street
Edinburgh EH2 3DH (for Scotland)
To view records, you can visit the Public Search Room between 8.30am and 4.30pm Monday to Friday

Public Search Room
St. Catherine's House
10 Kingsway
London WC2B 6JB

TELEPHONE ADVICE SERVICE

National Children's Home: 048 62 69229
    9.30–4.30 Tuesdays
Dr Barnardo's: 081 551 0011
    12.30–4.30 Wednesdays
NORCAP: 0865 750554
    10.00–4.00 Mon/Wed/Friday
Inter-country Adoption Helpline: 071 226 7666
    10.00–4.00 Weekdays
Family Care: 031 225 3666
    9.30–5.00 Weekdays
Scottish Adoption Advice Service: 041 339 0772
    2.00 – 5.00 Weekdays
    6.30–9.00 Weekdays

Useful Books for Adopted Children

I am Adopted, S. Lapsley, The Bodley Head. For very small children.
Robert goes to Fetch a Sister, D. Edwards and C. Dinan, Methuen. For children 3–7 years.
Susan and Gordon Adopt a Baby, J. Freudberg and T. Geiss, Random House. For children 4–7 years. (Sesame Street characters.)
Why Was I Adopted, C. Livingstone, Angus & Robertson. For children 5–10 years.
The Paddington Books, Michael Bond, Collins. All these books demonstrate how Paddington adjusts to living with a new family.

Index

abused children, 34, 112, 155–9
adolescents, 74–5, 101, 120–31
   case histories, 122–5, 126–30
   fostering, 121
   regression, 126
   talking about adoption, 200–2
adoption agencies, 24–5
   costs of adoption, 78–9
   finding a child, 62–4
   home studies, 37
   inter-country adoption, 166, 172, 175
   official assessments, 48–65
   tracing birth parents, 210
   see also local authority Social Services Departments
adoption allowances, 82–5, 134, 139
Adoption Contact Register, 208, 210
adoption panels, 60–1, 230
advertisements, 63–4
affection, indiscriminate, 113
age:
   adolescents, 74–5
   adoptive parents, 29–31
   children already in family, 31
   children available for adoption, 67–8
   foster parents, 221
aggression, 116–17, 125

AIDS babies, 72–3
allowances:
   adoption, 82–5, 134, 139
   child, 79
   foster care, 231
   maternity, 79–80
altruism, 13–16
assessments:
   official, 48–65
   personal, 37–47
attachment problems, 113
attitudes, personal assessment, 38–40

babies, 93–9
   advantages, 94–5
   AIDS, 72–3
   case histories, 97–9
   disadvantages, 95–6
   inter-country adoption, 202–3
   talking about adoption, 195–7
bedrooms, 88–9
bereavement, 17–19, 72–3, 133
birth certificates, 208, 210
birth parents:
   answering questions about, 198–200
   giving up babies, 93–4
   keeping in touch with, 205–6
   meeting adoptive parents, 93
   tracing, 207–18

tracing in inter-country adoption, 202
black children:
    fostering, 230
    inter-racial adoption, 149–54
    see also inter-country adoption; mixed-race children
bonding, 176–84
books:
    about prospective parents, 52–3
    telling child about adoption, 198, 201–2
breakdown of placements, 185–92
British Agency for Adoption and Fostering (BAAF), 23, 62–3, 231
Bulgaria, 166

child allowance, 79
clothes, 89
counselling, tracing birth parents, 209, 210

death, 17–19, 46, 72–3, 86, 133
Department of Health, 168–9
deprived children, 75–6, 100
disabled children, 70–2, 132–7
    allowances, 134
    deciding factors, 132–4
    fostering, 135, 231
    respite care, 135
    support network, 135
disruption meetings, 190–1
divide and rule, 112
divorce, 174
documentation:
    'Form E', 207
    inter-country adoption, 167–9, 172, 202

employment, 41–2, 140
entry clearance, inter-country adoption, 169–71, 173
expectations:
    in early days of adoption, 177, 178, 179
    personal assessment, 46–7
experience:
    personal assessment, 43–4
    reasons for adopting, 22–3

faecal soiling, 117
family groups, 69–70
    adoption allowances, 83
    advantages, 138–9
    case histories, 142–8
    disadvantages, 139–42
filling gaps, reasons for adopting, 19–21
finances:
    adoption allowances, 82–5, 134, 139
    child allowance, 79
    costs of adopting, 78–9
    day-to-day costs, 87–90
    disabled children, 134
    foster care, 85, 222, 231–2
    inter-country adoption, 167, 168, 172–4
    maternity allowance, 79–80
    personal status, 31–2
    private fostering, 229
    settling-in grants, 85
    sibling groups, 139
    wills, 86
finding a child, 61–5
flexibility, 39–40
Foreign Office, 168
'Form E', 207
foster parents:
    adopting children, 121
    allowances, 85, 222
    contested cases, 78–9
    disabled children, 135
    how to become, 227–31
    own children, 224–5

INDEX

reasons for being, 221–6
taking over children from, 177
friendships, 125–6, 200

General Register Office, 208
God-parents, 201
grandparents, 45, 122, 205
grief, 18
guardians, 86
guilt, 185–6

Hepatitis B, 73–4
HIV, 72–3, 170
Home Office, 169
home study, 51–60
   forms, 54–8
   foster parents, 230
   inter-country adoption, 166, 167, 168
   intimate questions, 53–9
   personal assessment, 37–47
   supporting reports, 52–3
   withholding information from, 35
homosexual couples, 28–9
honeymoon period, 109–10, 133–14
humour, 40
hydrocephalus, 70–2
hyperactivity, 116–17

illness, 34–5, 69
infertility, 11–13, 49, 53, 93
information meetings, 48–9
insurance policies, 87
inter-country adoption, 4, 163–75
   black children, 151
   procedures, 166–75
   support team, 191–2
   talking about adoption, 202–4
   tracing birth parents, 202
inter-racial adoption, 149–54
interviews, 49, 52, 53, 59

Jews, 24

lawyers' fees, 78, 172, 173
legalized documents, 168, 172
lesbian couples, 28–9
lifestyle, 31–2
   adjusting to changes, 176–7
   adopting sibling groups, 140–1
   personal assessment, 41–3
   social status, 75–6
link workers, 189, 223
local authority Social Services Departments:
   adoption allowances, 82–5
   applying for adoption, 24–5
   costs of adoption, 78–9
   finding a child, 62–4
   foster parents, 227, 230
   inter-country adoption, 166, 167, 172, 175, 191–2
   inter-racial adoption, 68, 150
   official assessments, 48–65
   private fostering, 229
   tracing birth parents, 210
long term fostering, 227, 228–9
love, learning to give and receive, 176–84

marriage, 25, 34
marriage certificates, 210
married couples, 25
maternity allowance and leave, 79–82
medical conditions, 34–5
medical reports, 52, 167
medicine, private, 87
mixed-race children, 5, 68
   cultural identity, 150–1
   fostering, 230
   official policies, 22–3
   see also inter-country adoption; inter-racial adoption
Moldava, 170–1

motives for adoption, 11–23
mutilation, 117

night-time problems, 118
NORCAP, 210
notarized documents, 168, 172

offenders, 33–4
official assessment, 48–65
older children *see* adolescents; school-age children
over-competency, 114–15

panels, adoption, 60–1, 230
Parent and Parent Information on Adoptive Services (PPIAS), 23, 62, 63, 84
parental love, 179–84
passports, 169–70
permanent fostering, 228–9
personal assessment, 37–47
personal circumstances, 33–6
personal experience, reasons for adopting, 16
personal qualities, 32–3
personal status, 31–2
please, desire to, 113–114
police checks, 52, 59, 167
practical motives, 17
prejudice, racial, 151, 204
preliminary interviews, 49
preparation groups, 49–51
presents, 88
pride, 40
private fostering, 227, 229
private medical schemes, 87
psychiatric illness, 34–5, 69, 117

references, 52, 59
regression, 89–90, 111–12, 126
religion, 24
respite care, 135
roles, parents, 40
Roman Catholic Church, 24

Romania, 4, 15, 67, 70–2, 105–6, 116, 163–4, 166, 169, 170, 174, 178, 194
Romanian Adoption Committee, 169

St. Catherine's House, 210
schizophrenia, 69
school-age children, 107–19
　case histories, 113, 114, 115
　honeymoon period, 109–10
　problems, 109–18
　talking about adoption, 197–200
　see also adolescents
second-hand clothes and equipment, 89, 90
self-awareness, lack of, 115–16
self-image, adolescents, 125
self-mutilation, 117
separation, 34
settling-in grants, 85
sexuality, home study, 53
sexually abused children, 53, 112, 155–9
short-term fostering, 227–8
sibling groups *see* family groups
single parents:
　fostering, 222–3
　men, 28
　support network, 45–6
　women, 26–8
sleep problems, 118
Social Services Departments *see* local authority Social Services Departments
social status, 75–7
social workers:
　advertisements, 63–4
　breakdown of placements, 186, 188, 190–1
　and fostering, 223, 224, 230
　home study, 52, 53
　inter-country adoption, 171–2

preliminary interview, 49
support team, 189–90
tracing birth parents, 211
soiling, faecal, 117
special needs children:
adoption allowances, 83
see also disabled children
specialist foster carers, 231
status:
foster parents' children, 224
personal, 31–2
social, 75–6
STORK, 166
storybooks, telling child about adoption, 198, 201–2
support networks, 44–6
support team, social workers, 189–90

tantrums, 111
teenagers *see* adolescents
telling child about adoption, 193–205
temporary fostering, 227–8
testing time, 110–11

toddlers, 93, 100–6
advantages, 100–1
case histories, 102–4, 105–6
disadvantages, 101–2
talking about adoption, 195–7
tolerance, 38–9
toys, 88, 89
tracing birth parents, 207–18
transracial adoption *see* inter-racial adoption
Turkey, 171, 172

unmarried couples, 25–6
USSR, 170–1

visas, 169–70

waiting lists, 49, 67–8
wills, 86
work, 41–2, 140